Your Start with GenAI

Generative AI (GenAI) has rapidly transformed the business landscape, moving from early enthusiasm to widespread adoption across sectors. Organizations now leverage its capabilities to boost efficiency, drive innovation, and create personalized customer experiences. While initial excitement led to inflated expectations, GenAI's sustained momentum shows its resilience and growing maturity.

This shift from hype to practical use marks a turning point. GenAI's ability to streamline workflows, innovate products and services, and enhance customer engagement makes it a critical differentiator in today's competitive market. As businesses face rapid change, GenAI stands out as a catalyst for transformation and value creation.

This book guides decision-makers, IT managers, and business leaders through the strategic adoption of GenAI. It provides a roadmap to identify high-value use cases, prepare organizations, and scale GenAI for impact. By demystifying GenAI and offering actionable frameworks, this book helps readers harness its potential to drive innovation, efficiency, and competitive advantage in an evolving digital world.

The GenAI Hype

In 2024, Generative AI (GenAI) is entering a phase of reassessment and recalibration after a period of intense initial enthusiasm. During 2022 and 2023, GenAI captivated both public attention and substantial investment, with early adopters and tech visionaries championing its transformative potential across nearly every industry. This period, characterized by "inflated expectations," placed GenAI under a spotlight, where its capabilities were frequently viewed as revolutionary. By 2024, however, GenAI's position has shifted to what Gartner describes as the "trough of disillusionment," a stage in the hype cycle where early excitement often gives way to a more realistic appraisal of both its strengths and limitations (ManageEngine, 2024).

Despite this moderated outlook, GenAI adoption has not waned; it has instead become more focused and strategic. A McKinsey survey reports that nearly 65% of organizations now regularly incorporate GenAI into their operations – a substantial increase from the previous year. Sectors such as marketing, sales, and product development have particularly benefitted, with organizations citing measurable improvements in cost reduction and operational efficiency. Many businesses are now concentrating on embedding GenAI into existing workflows with a clear focus on value generation rather than exploratory use (McKinsey & Company, 2024).

Figure 1 - Hype of GenAI

This rise in targeted GenAI adoption has also ignited industry-wide conversations about its sustainability and risks of overinvestment. While some experts continue to advocate for GenAI's transformative impact, others caution against unrealistic expectations, likening the current hype to previous technology bubbles. Analysts point out that while GenAI is impressive, its immediate revenue potential may not always align with the scale of investment, emphasizing the need for a balanced, realistic perspective on its financial sustainability (Le Monde, 2024).

In essence, 2024 marks a turning point for GenAI as it moves from an experimental phase to one that prioritizes practical applications and measurable outcomes. Organizations that have invested in GenAI are now focused on identifying areas where it adds real value, assessing costs against long-term benefits, and aligning its use with strategic objectives. This shift reflects a more mature approach to GenAI, where the goal is no longer about being at the cutting edge but about integrating GenAI as a sustainable component of business processes. As businesses move beyond the initial hype, they are recognizing that GenAI's true potential lies in a measured, strategic adoption focused on delivering lasting value.

How to read this book

This book is a step-by-step guide for unlocking Generative AI's (GenAI) potential in your organization. Tailored for decision-makers, IT managers, and business leaders, it offers practical strategies for driving real business value through GenAI. Here's how to get the most out of it:

Start with the Foundations: Begin with the introductory chapters to understand GenAI's transformative potential, industry impact, and alignment with strategic business goals.

Dive into Real-World Use Cases: Study detailed examples across industries to see how GenAI creates tangible value. Use these insights to identify relevant opportunities within your own organization.

Leverage Practical Frameworks and Tools: Use tools like the GenAI Use Case Canvas to identify, evaluate, and prioritize initiatives. Ensure your projects align with business goals and offer high potential value.

Follow the Implementation Roadmap: Navigate the steps from use case selection to scaling enterprise-wide adoption. Focus on resource allocation, governance, and addressing common challenges.

Adapt and Engage: Adapt the strategies to your organization's needs. Involve key stakeholders and build cross-departmental collaboration to foster buy-in and alignment.

By following this approach, you will be equipped to turn GenAI potential into scalable business value and drive long-term success.

About the Authors

Dr. Sven-Erik Willrich and Lars Willrich are brothers with passion for (Gen)AI and empowering companies to become data-driven.

Dr. Sven-Erik Willrich is a Data Management expert with a strong industry / consultancy background. He frequently shares his expertise through lectures, articles, and industry engagements.

Lars Willrich (MBA), as Head of Data and AI at a global consulting firm, leads business development and advises clients on leveraging GenAI, driving forward innovative, data-centric solutions.

Where GenAI Crates Value in Business

Generative AI (GenAI) is set to deliver substantial benefits across numerous business functions, with its economic impact projected to vary by sector. According to McKinsey, GenAI could contribute an additional $2.6 trillion to $4.4 trillion annually across industries, increasing the value derived from non-generative AI and analytics by 15 to 40 percent (McKinsey, 2023).

The business functions expected to benefit most from GenAI, along with their potential economic impact, include:

- **Marketing and Sales**: GenAI can streamline content creation, personalize marketing strategies, and enhance customer engagement. This function could see an impact ranging from 0.9% to 4.7% of industry revenue, depending on the sector (McKinsey, 2023).

- **Customer Operations**: By optimizing customer interactions and support services, GenAI can enhance both efficiency and satisfaction. The potential impact in this area is estimated between 0.5% and 4.0% of industry revenue (McKinsey, 2023).

- **Product Research and Development (R&D)**: GenAI enables faster innovation cycles and more efficient product development processes. The expected impact in R&D ranges from 0.6% to 2.4% of industry revenue (McKinsey, 2023).

- **Software Engineering**: GenAI aids in code generation and debugging, significantly boosting development efficiency. This function could experience an impact between 0.7% and 9.3% of industry revenue, particularly in technology-intensive sectors (McKinsey, 2023).

These numbers highlight GenAI's capacity to transform key business functions, enhancing productivity and fostering innovation across diverse industries (McKinsey, 2023).

In today's fast-evolving digital landscape, Generative AI (GenAI) is reshaping the business world, sparking transformation across industries. More than just a technological advancement, GenAI introduces new avenues for value creation that extend beyond traditional automation or analytics. It enables businesses to reimagine customer experiences, streamline operations, innovate in products and services, and even uncover novel revenue streams. In the evolving landscape, Generative AI (GenAI) drives value across three critical dimensions: *Operational Efficiency*, *Customer Engagement*, and *Products & Services*. These areas align closely with Jan Marco Leimeister's digitalization framework - *Digital Processes*, *Digital Users/Consumers*, and *Smart Products and Services* – see Figure 2. Each of which reflects how organizations can integrate technology to achieve a holistic digital transformation.

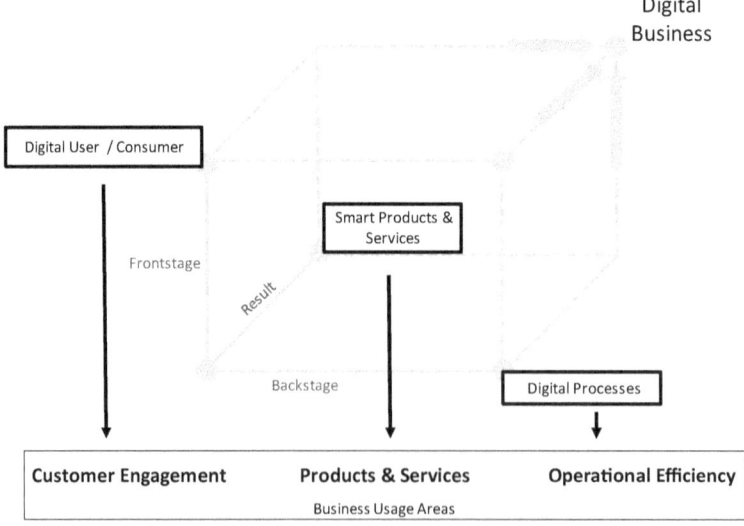

Figure 2 - Three Dimensions of Digitalization based on Leimeister, 2021

The following sections provide a deeper look into these dimensions and explore how GenAI enhances them. Through practical examples and strategic insights, we'll see how GenAI enables transformative shifts in efficiency, customer interaction, and product innovation – establishing it as a vital tool for modernizing and future-proofing businesses.

1. **Operational Efficiency (Digital Processes)**: GenAI optimizes internal workflows and back-office processes, directly enhancing Leimeister's *Digital Processes* dimension. By automating repetitive tasks, reducing errors, and providing predictive analytics, GenAI improves productivity, accelerates decision-making, and supports smarter, more agile operations.

2. **Customer Engagement (Digital Users/Consumers)**: In Leimeister's framework, *Digital Users/Consumers* emphasizes a customer-centric approach, transforming how organizations interact with their audiences. GenAI powers this transformation through hyper-personalization, intelligent chatbots, and predictive insights, enabling companies to engage customers with relevant, responsive interactions that drive loyalty and satisfaction.

3. **Products & Services (Smart Products and Services)**: Leimeister's dimension of *Smart Products and Services* reflects the potential of digital technologies to create intelligent, adaptive offerings. GenAI allows companies to innovate by embedding AI into products and services, tailoring them to customer needs and accelerating time-to-market. This capability is particularly valuable in industries where customization and innovation are critical to staying competitive.

By strategically integrating GenAI within these three dimensions, organizations can not only optimize their existing operations but also enhance customer relationships and bring advanced, AI-driven products to market. This comprehensive approach to digitalization positions businesses to thrive in a competitive, data-driven world and fully realize the benefits of digital transformation.

To fully leverage the transformative power of GenAI, it's essential to integrate these three dimensions – Operational Efficiency, Customer Engagement, and Products & Services – across the entire enterprise value chain. This holistic approach not only enhances individual areas but also drives cohesive improvements across all primary and supportive functions, maximizing the impact of digitalization efforts, see Figure 3. While every company's value chain is unique, here's an example of how GenAI can optimize various phases.

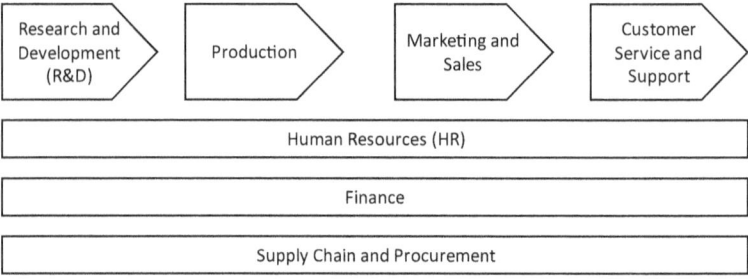

Figure 3 - Example Enterprise Value Chain

Primary Functions

These functions are essential to a company's core operations and vary by industry, but typically include:

- **Research and Development (R&D):** where new products or services are conceived and developed. GenAI accelerates R&D by generating design prototypes, predicting outcomes, and supporting iterative testing.

- **Production:** where products or services are manufactured or assembled. GenAI optimizes production by forecasting demand patterns and detecting quality issues early through predictive analytics.

- **Marketing and Sales:** where offerings are promoted and delivered to market. GenAI enhances marketing efforts through personalized content generation and customer segmentation for targeted outreach.

- **Customer Service and Support:** where companies engage with customers post-sale to build loyalty. GenAI enables 24/7 support through intelligent chatbots, personalized responses, and sentiment analysis.

Supportive Functions

These functions enable and sustain primary operations across departments and include:

- **Human Resources (HR):** managing recruitment, development, and retention of talent. GenAI streamlines HR processes by automating candidate screening, improving employee engagement through personalized onboarding, and providing insights for workforce planning.

- **Finance:** overseeing budgets, forecasting, and compliance. GenAI Improves financial planning with predictive analytics, accelerates reporting, and enhances accuracy in forecasting.

- **Supply Chain and Procurement:** handling inventory, logistics, and supplier relationships. GenAI optimizes supply chain management through real-time demand forecasting, risk assessment, and automation of order tracking.

Through these examples, we see how GenAI can support both primary and supportive functions, enabling efficiencies and innovation across all stages of the value chain.

Structure of GenAI Use Cases

This chapter introduces the **GenAI Use Case Taxonomy** and the **GenAI Use Case Canvas** to provide a consistent framework for each use case in this book. The taxonomy offers a classification system that organizes use cases by business impact, technical capability, interaction level, and data sensitivity, helping readers understand the strategic positioning of each application. The canvas serves as a structured template, covering business objectives, technical details, operational needs, and data considerations, ensuring a thorough view of each use case's potential.
Each use case is presented in alignment with the taxonomy and structured according to the canvas, giving readers a clear, comprehensive framework for evaluating and implementing GenAI solutions.

A GenAI Taxonomy

Taxonomies organize information into a structured framework, enabling classification and understanding of complex subjects by grouping related elements into categories. In the context of Generative AI (GenAI), a well-defined taxonomy helps decision-makers, IT managers, and professionals systematically classify and analyze various AI applications, allowing for more strategic alignment, efficient resource allocation, and compliance with regulatory standards.

The **GenAI Use Case Taxonomy** introduces a framework specifically tailored for classifying GenAI applications – see Figure 4. It offers a multidimensional approach to categorizing use cases based on business relevance, capabilities, interaction modes, and data sensitivity. This taxonomy aids organizations in assessing use cases' operational impact, complexity, and data requirements. Below is a description of each taxonomy dimension and its values.

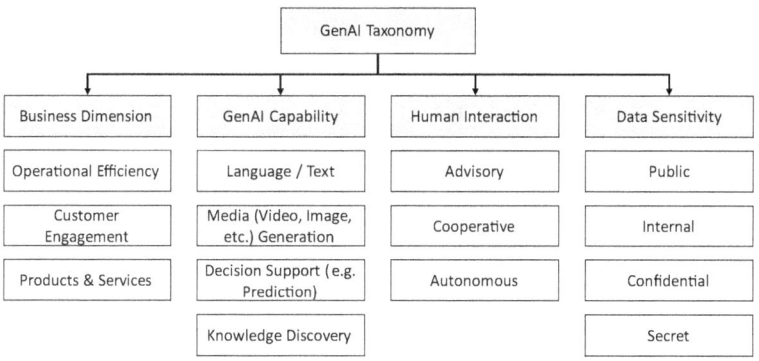

Figure 4 - GenAI Use Case Taxonomy

Business Dimension

Description: This dimension categorizes GenAI use cases based on their contribution to business goals, either by optimizing internal operations or by enhancing products and services offered to customers.

Guiding Question: Is the primary goal of this GenAI use case to improve operational efficiency or to enhance products and services for customers?

- **Operational Efficiency**: Focuses on improving internal processes, reducing costs, and increasing productivity.
- **Products & Services**: Aims at enhancing or creating customer-facing products and services, contributing to business growth and differentiation.

GenAI Capability

Description: This dimension identifies the specific capabilities or output types of the GenAI application, such as generating language, media, decision support, or extracting knowledge.

Guiding Question: What core capability does this GenAI use case provide to address the business need?

- **Language Generation**: Produces written content, such as text generation, summarization, and translation.
- **Media (Video, Image, etc.) Generation**: Creates visual or audio content, including images, videos, and music.

- **Decision Support (e.g., Prediction)**: Provides predictive insights and assists in decision-making.
- **Knowledge Discovery**: Extracts valuable information and insights from large data sets.

Human Interaction

Description: This dimension defines the level of human interaction required with the GenAI application, from advisory roles to full autonomy.

Guiding Question: *What level of interaction or collaboration is required between the GenAI solution and its human users?*

- **Advisory**: Provides guidance and recommendations but does not take direct action.
- **Cooperative**: Works alongside humans, enhancing tasks through collaboration or assistance.
- **Autonomous**: Operates independently, performing tasks without human intervention.

Data Sensitivity

Description: This dimension assesses the sensitivity level of the data used in the GenAI use case, ranging from public to highly confidential or classified information.

Guiding Question: *What level of data sensitivity is involved in this GenAI use case, and how restricted is its access?*

- **Public**: Uses publicly accessible data without privacy or confidentiality concerns.
- **Internal**: Restricted to internal organizational data, requiring controlled access.
- **Confidential**: Handles sensitive data where confidentiality is essential for privacy or business protection.
- **Secret**: Involves highly sensitive or classified data with strict access and security requirements.

This taxonomy helps organizations systematically assess and classify GenAI use cases, providing clarity on their business relevance, interaction needs, capabilities, and data requirements.

Each use case presented in this book is systematically classified along this GenAI Use Case Taxonomy. This structured approach provides readers with a clear understanding of each use case's business relevance, technical capabilities, interaction level, and data requirements, enabling informed decision-making and strategic implementation within their organizations.

The GenAI Use Case Canvas

The **GenAI Use Case Canvas** is designed to capture the essential elements of a GenAI application in a clear, structured format and is shown in Figure 5. It includes core fields for evaluating each use case's business purpose, implementation approach, and expected outcomes.

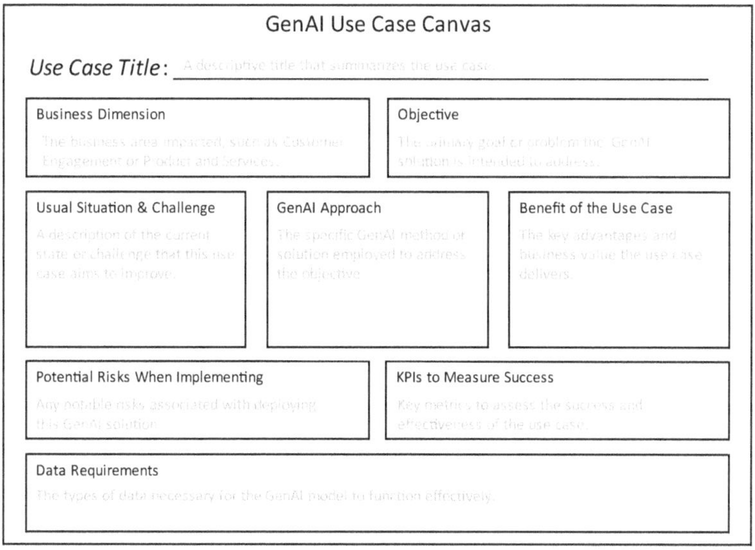

Figure 5 - GenAI Use Case Canvas

Additional fields, such as use case owner, responsible department, creation and last update dates, and current status (from design to production), may be included to enhance tracking and accountability, but the canvas should remain practical and not overly complex.

Use Case Title: A descriptive title that summarizes the use case.
Example: "Customer Service Chatbot for Retail Inquiries"

Business Dimension: The business area impacted, such as Customer Engagement or Product and Services.
Example: "Customer Engagement"

Objective: The primary goal or problem the GenAI solution is intended to address.
Example: "Reduce response time for customer inquiries by automating common queries."

Usual Situation & Challenge: A description of the current state or challenge that this use case aims to improve.
Example: "Customers experience long wait times due to high inquiry volumes, impacting satisfaction."

GenAI Approach: The specific GenAI method or solution employed to address the objective.
Example: "Deploy an AI chatbot capable of answering frequently asked questions in real-time."

Benefit of the Use Case: The key advantages and business value the use case delivers.
Example: "Improves customer experience by reducing response times and freeing up human agents for complex inquiries."

Potential Risks When Implementing: Any notable risks associated with deploying this GenAI solution.
Example: "Potential risk of incorrect responses impacting customer trust."

KPIs to Measure Success: Key metrics to assess the success and effectiveness of the use case.
Example: "Customer satisfaction score (CSAT), average response time, inquiry resolution rate."

Data Requirements: The types of data necessary for the GenAI model to function effectively.
Example: "Historical customer inquiries and responses, product information database."

The **GenAI Use Case Canvas** serves as a practical tool for documenting, evaluating, and communicating each GenAI application within an organization. By covering the essential aspects – from objectives and challenges to risks and success metrics – it ensures all stakeholders have a clear, consistent understanding of the purpose and requirements of each use case. This canvas helps align GenAI initiatives with business goals, prioritize resources effectively, and monitor implementation progress.

List of 30 GenAI Use Cases

In in chapters, we present investigated GenAI Use Case using the GenAI Use Case Canvas to explore high-impact use cases across four major industries:

1. **Manufacturing**: Focused on producing goods through processes like machining, assembly, and automation, often incorporating advanced technologies like robotics and AI to improve efficiency and product quality.
2. **Financial**: Encompasses services related to managing money, including banking, insurance, investments, and asset management, with a strong emphasis on data security, compliance, and digital transactions.
3. **Healthcare**: Provides medical services, pharmaceuticals, and wellness solutions aimed at improving patient outcomes, often leveraging technology for diagnostics, treatment, and patient care management.
4. **Public**: Includes government and public sector services focused on maintaining public welfare, infrastructure, and regulatory frameworks, often prioritizing transparency, accessibility, and community impact.

Within each industry, we examine use cases focused on the already mentioned three business dimensions:

1. **Products and Services**: Use cases that enable new product offerings, optimize existing services, and drive product innovation.

2. **Customer Engagement**: Use cases that elevate customer experiences, improve service quality, and deepen customer relationships.

3. **Operational Efficiency**: Use cases that streamline internal processes, reduce costs, and enhance productivity.

In this book, **30 GenAI use cases** are presented using the **GenAI Use Case Canvas** format, providing a structured view of each case's objectives, approach, and expected outcomes. Each use case is classified according to the **GenAI Use Case Taxonomy**. Additionally, each use case is mapped to a **Business Dimension** – operational efficiency, customer engagement, or products and services.

Products & Services

The following table shows shows 10 GenAI Use Cases from Products & Services.

#	Use Case Title
1	Real-Time Equipment Health Monitoring
2	Interactive Language Translation
3	Personalized Financial Dashboard
4	Virtual Health Coach
5	Visual Inventory Management System
6	Public Process Navigator
7	Investment Advisor
8	Car Assistent
9	Diagnostic Assistent
10	Individualized education assistent

Customer Engagement

The following table shows shows 10 GenAI Use Cases from Customer Engagement.

#	Use Case Title
11	Customer Sentiment Analysis
12	Intelligent Service Request Routing
13	AI Health Chatbot

#	Use Case Title
14	Localized Customer Service Assistant
15	Personalized Investment Insights
16	Virtual Product Specialist
17	Customer Profile Enrichment
18	Feedback-Driven Ad Creation
19	Automated Customer Survey Generation
20	Social Media Response Automation

Operational Efficiency

The following table shows shows 10 GenAI Use Cases from Operational Efficiency.

#	Use Case Title
21	Financial Report Analysis Assistant
22	Automated Literature Review for R&D
23	Data Protection Audit Automation
24	Contract Terms Extraction
25	Error Log Analysis & Summarization
27	Automatic Meeting Transcript Generator
26	Code Completion & Suggestion Tool
28	Invoice Assistent
29	Internal Chatbot Knowledge Base
30	Technical Documentation Creation and Management

10

of GenAI Use Cases for
Products & Services

#1 Real-Time Equipment Health Monitoring

Business Dimension	Products & Services
Industry	Manufacturing
Objective	Real-time detection of equipment issues through sound analysis.

Usual Situation & Challenge

Manufacturers often rely on reactive maintenance and manual inspections, resulting in unplanned downtime and high repair costs. Traditional systems may miss subtle audio-based anomalies or degrade with sensor wear.

GenAI Approach

GenAI models analyze real-time equipment audio data, identifying anomalies and predicting potential failures using deep learning techniques. This helps shift maintenance to a proactive approach, improving machine uptime and efficiency.

- Real-time anomaly detection and alerts
- Adaptive learning for new machine behaviors
- Integrates with existing monitoring systems

Benefit of the Use Case

Increased equipment uptime, reduced maintenance costs, and improved safety benefit plant managers, maintenance teams, and overall operational efficiency.

Potential Risks by Implementing the Use Case

- High initial setup and training costs
- Data privacy concerns around proprietary processes
- False positives or missed anomalies

KPIs to Measure the Success of the Use Case

- Reduction in unplanned downtime=
- Increase in mean time between failures (MTBF)

Data Requirements

- Real-time data capturing sound vibrations and frequencies
- Data to train and calibrate anomaly detection models
- Baseline performance data for normal operation patterns

Selected GenAI Taxonomy Dimensions

The following taxonomy, also introduced in Figure 4 - GenAI Use Case Taxonomy, classifies this Use Case along the relevant dimensions.

Taxonomy				
Business Dimension	Operational Efficiency	Customer Engagement		Products & Services
GenAI Capability	Language / Text	Media	Decision Support	Knowledge Discovery
Human Interaction	Advisory	Cooperative		Autonomous
Data Sensitvity	Public	Internal	Confidential	Secret

#2 | Interactive Language Translation

Business Dimension	Products & Services
Industry	Public
Objective	Real-time multilingual communication in public services

Usual Situation & Challenge

Language barriers hinder effective communication between public service representatives and non-native speakers, reducing accessibility and customer satisfaction. Traditional translation tools often lack context and nuance, impacting service delivery.

GenAI Approach

GenAI models provide **real-time, context-aware translations** that maintain nuance and specific cultural understanding, ensuring smoother interactions and greater inclusivity.

- Contextualized responses for complex interactions
- Multimodal translation options (voice/text)
- Continuous learning for accuracy improvements

Benefit of the Use Case

Improves **service accessibility** and customer satisfaction for multilingual users, enabling more inclusive public services. **Public service agents** benefit from better engagement outcomes.

Potential Risks by Implementing the Use Case

- Language bias/errors impacting service quality
- Data privacy issues with sensitive communication
- Dependence on technology may require redundancy planning

KPIs to Measure the Success of the Use Case

- User satisfaction scores for multilingual interactions
- Response time improvement for language-based requests

Data Requirements

- Language-specific datasets for training GenAI models
- Service interaction data for real-world contextual adaptation
- Cultural/contextual nuance data to refine responses

Selected GenAI Taxonomy Dimensions

The following taxonomy, also introduced in Figure 4 - GenAI Use Case Taxonomy, classifies this Use Case along the relevant dimensions.

Taxonomy				
Business Dimension	Operational Efficiency	Customer Engagement		Products & Services
GenAI Capability	Language / Text	Media	Decision Support	Knowledge Discovery
Human Interaction	Advisory	Cooperative		Autonomous
Data Sensitvity	Public	Internal	Confidential	Secret

#3 Personalized Financial Dashboard

Business Dimension	Products & Services
Industry	Financial
Objective	Tailor financial insights to individual customer needs

Usual Situation & Challenge

Financial institutions often provide generic dashboards, failing to address **unique customer needs** and behaviors, resulting in low engagement and satisfaction among users.

GenAI Approach

The solution leverages **GenAI-driven analytics** to create personalized dashboards that generate tailored recommendations, predictive financial insights, and alerts for individual customers based on their spending and goals.

- Personalized recommendations based on transaction patterns
- Predictive analytics to highlight potential risks or opportunities
- Goal-based suggestions for budgeting and savings

Benefit of the Use Case

Increased **customer satisfaction and engagement** by offering relevant financial insights, benefiting both customers and financial institutions by driving loyalty and better customer behavior.

Potential Risks by Implementing the Use Case

- Data privacy concerns
- Algorithmic biases impacting recommendations
- Security risks in personalized data handling

KPIs to Measure the Success of the Use Case

- Increase in customer engagement rates
- Growth in customer retention and satisfaction

Data Requirements

- **Transaction Data**: Customer purchase and spending patterns
- **User Demographic Data**: Age, income level, etc., for tailored insights
- **Financial Goals and Preferences**: User-provided data to personalize dashboard features

Selected GenAI Taxonomy Dimensions

The following taxonomy, also introduced in Figure 4 - GenAI Use Case Taxonomy, classifies this Use Case along the relevant dimensions.

Taxonomy				
Business Dimension	Operational Efficiency	Customer Engagement		Products & Services
GenAI Capability	Language / Text	Media	Decision Support	Knowledge Discovery
Human Interaction	Advisory	Cooperative		Autonomous
Data Sensitvity	Public	Internal	Confidential	Secret

#4 | Virtual Health Coach

Business Dimension	Products & Services
Industry	Health
Objective	Provide tailored health and fitness recommendations via AI.

Usual Situation & Challenge

Many individuals lack **personalized fitness guidance** due to high costs, limited access to professional coaches, or busy schedules. This leads to inconsistent routines and limited progress toward health goals.

GenAI Approach

A Virtual Health Coach powered by GenAI offers **personalized fitness and health plans** by analyzing user data, preferences, and health metrics in real-time. Through AI-generated **recommendations, progress tracking**, it individualizes plans.

- Delivers tailored fitness routines based on user profile and goals
- Provides ongoing motivation via AI-generated messages and feedback
- Tracks and adjusts recommendations using real-time data and user input

Benefit of the Use Case

Users receive **tailored, accessible health coaching** that adapts to their progress and goals, driving **better health outcomes** and engagement with wellness routines. Reduces need for expensive personal trainers.

Potential Risks by Implementing the Use Case

- Data privacy concerns due to health information handling
- Bias in recommendations if data is not representative
- Over-reliance on AI without professional input

KPIs to Measure the Success of the Use Case

- User engagement and retention rates
- Improvement in user health metrics (e.g., fitness, weight goals)

Data Requirements

- Demographics, lifestyle preferences, goals
- Physical activity, weight, nutrition intake
- Continuous user input on plan effectiveness

Selected GenAI Taxonomy Dimensions

The following taxonomy, also introduced in Figure 4 - GenAI Use Case Taxonomy, classifies this Use Case along the relevant dimensions.

Taxonomy				
Business Dimension	Operational Efficiency	Customer Engagement		Products & Services
GenAI Capability	Language / Text	Media	Decision Support	Knowledge Discovery
Human Interaction	Advisory	Cooperative		Autonomous
Data Sensitvity	Public	Internal	Confidential	Secret

#5 Visual Inventory Management System

Business Dimension	Products & Services
Industry	Manufacturing
Objective	Optimize inventory tracking using real-time image recognition.

Usual Situation & Challenge

Manual inventory processes lead to **inaccurate stock counts, slow updates**, and **mismanagement** of supply levels, causing **operational delays** and **waste**. This impacts overall productivity and cost efficiency.

GenAI Approach

GenAI leverages **image recognition** to automate stock tracking and **detect discrepancies in inventory levels** through real-time visual analysis, reducing manual errors and delays.

- Automates inventory data capture using image recognition.
- Alerts for **discrepancies** between physical and logged inventory.
- Integrates with existing inventory software for real-time updates.

Benefit of the Use Case

The system improves **accuracy, speeds up inventory operations,** and **reduces costs** by minimizing human errors. **Supply chain managers and operators** benefit from a streamlined process.

Potential Risks by Implementing the Use Case

- Potential **privacy issues** with camera usage in sensitive areas.
- **Integration challenges** with existing systems.
- Risk of **misclassifications** affecting inventory data.

KPIs to Measure the Success of the Use Case

- Inventory accuracy rate improvement.
- **Reduction in time** to complete inventory audits.

Data Requirements

- **Image data** of inventory items (including different angles and conditions).
- **Historical inventory records** for training accuracy and detecting discrepancies.
- Location and stock-keeping unit (SKU) data to map items correctly.

Selected GenAI Taxonomy Dimensions

The following taxonomy, also introduced in Figure 4 - GenAI Use Case Taxonomy, classifies this Use Case along the relevant dimensions.

Taxonomy				
Business Dimension	Operational Efficiency	Customer Engagement		Products & Services
GenAI Capability	Language / Text	Media	Decision Support	Knowledge Discovery
Human Interaction	Advisory	Cooperative		Autonomous
Data Sensitvity	Public	Internal	Confidential	Secret

#6 | Public Process Navigator

Business Dimension	Products & Services
Industry	Public
Objective	Streamline citizens' navigation of complex public processes.

Usual Situation & Challenge

Citizens often face **confusing, fragmented public processes** with **bureaucratic delays, lack of clear guidance, and complex forms** that hinder timely and accurate completion of tasks.

GenAI Approach

A GenAI-powered assistant simplifies public process navigation by providing **contextual, natural language responses, form completion support, and personalized step-by-step guidance** to users, thereby reducing delays and confusion.

- Natural language responses for queries
- Tailored step-by-step process guides
- Pre-filling forms based on data input and context
- Proactive status updates and reminders

Benefit of the Use Case

Reduces time and complexity for citizens, improving **public satisfaction and trust** in government services; **public officials' workload** decreases with fewer errors and streamlined processes.

Potential Risks by Implementing the Use Case

- Data privacy concerns if sensitive citizen data is not managed securely
- Risk of biased guidance without robust training data
- Misinterpretation of complex legal information

KPIs to Measure the Success of the Use Case

- Reduction in process completion times for citizens
- Increase in citizen satisfaction scores

Data Requirements

- Citizen data, including personal identification and application history, to provide personalized guidance
- Process data from government workflows to map accurate navigation paths
- Historical queries and feedback data to improve GenAI responses over time

Selected GenAI Taxonomy Dimensions

The following taxonomy, also introduced in Figure 4 - GenAI Use Case Taxonomy, classifies this Use Case along the relevant dimensions.

Taxonomy				
Business Dimension	Operational Efficiency	Customer Engagement		Products & Services
GenAI Capability	Language / Text	Media	Decision Support	Knowledge Discovery
Human Interaction	Advisory		Cooperative	Autonomous
Data Sensitvity	Public	Internal	Confidential	Secret

#7 | Investment Advisor

Business Dimension	Products & Services
Industry	Financial
Objective	Personalized investment strategy recommendations.

Usual Situation & Challenge

Investors often face **overwhelming complexity and information overload** when seeking investment strategies tailored to their needs. Traditional tools fail to provide **real-time contextual insights**, often resulting in generic advice or missed opportunities.

GenAI Approach

The Investment Advisor leverages **GenAI models for tailored recommendations** by analyzing vast datasets on market trends, individual risk tolerance, and investment goals. It provides personalized, **real-time strategy suggestions** using natural language processing and predictive modeling.

- Personalized investment strategy suggestions based on user data and goals
- Real-time market analysis and contextual recommendations
- Integration of user behavior analytics for adaptive strategies

Benefit of the Use Case

Investors receive **tailored and highly relevant strategies** in real-time, enhancing investment outcomes and overall satisfaction. **Financial institutions improve customer engagement** and drive loyalty.

Potential Risks by Implementing the Use Case

- Data privacy concerns
- Potential for biased recommendations
- Over-reliance on automated decisions

KPIs to Measure the Success of the Use Case

- Increase in customer portfolio performance
- Customer engagement and satisfaction scores

Data Requirements

- Historical market and asset performance data
- Customer risk tolerance and investment history
- Real-time market data for adaptive strategy generation

Selected GenAI Taxonomy Dimensions

The following taxonomy, also introduced in Figure 4 - GenAI Use Case Taxonomy, classifies this Use Case along the relevant dimensions.

Taxonomy				
Business Dimension	Operational Efficiency	Customer Engagement		Products & Services
GenAI Capability	Language / Text	Media	Decision Support	Knowledge Discovery
Human Interaction	Advisory	Cooperative		Autonomous
Data Sensitvity	Public	Internal	Confidential	Secret

#8 | Car Assistant

Business Dimension	Products & Services
Industry	Manufacturing
Objective	Assist drivers in operating and understanding their car in natural language.

Usual Situation & Challenge

Drivers often struggle with **complex vehicle features** and require **quick guidance** for troubleshooting or system settings, leading to **frustration** and **ineffective feature use**.

GenAI Approach

A Car Assistant leveraging GenAI enables **natural language interaction** to answer driver queries, explain functions, and provide **real-time guidance**. This involves:

- Contextual voice/text-based car operation help
- Personalized insights based on driving data
- Proactive alerts and recommendations for maintenance

Benefit of the Use Case

Enhanced user experience with intuitive car controls, **higher customer satisfaction**, and **better utilization of vehicle features** benefiting both drivers and car manufacturers.

Potential Risks by Implementing the Use Case

- Data privacy concerns
- Misinterpretation of user inputs
- Dependence on connectivity

KPIs to Measure the Success of the Use Case

- Customer satisfaction rate
- Feature engagement metrics

Data Requirements

- **User interaction data**: To improve personalized assistance and accuracy
- **Vehicle operational data**: For contextual guidance and maintenance alerts
- **Driving behavior data**: To tailor tips and safety suggestions

Selected GenAI Taxonomy Dimensions

The following taxonomy, also introduced in Figure 4 - GenAI Use Case Taxonomy, classifies this Use Case along the relevant dimensions.

Taxonomy				
Business Dimension	Operational Efficiency	Customer Engagement		Products & Services
GenAI Capability	Language / Text	Media	Decision Support	Knowledge Discovery
Human Interaction	Advisory	Cooperative		Autonomous
Data Sensitvity	Public	Internal	Confidential	Secret

#9 Diagnostic Assistant for Medical Imaging

Business Dimension	Products & Services
Industry	Health
Objective	Accelerate diagnostic accuracy using image-based AI assistance.

Usual Situation & Challenge

Clinicians face **high diagnostic workloads, complex imaging data interpretation, and potential human errors**. The process often demands significant time, contributing to patient wait times and diagnostic inconsistencies.

GenAI Approach

AI models **analyze medical images**, offering diagnostic suggestions by detecting patterns and anomalies in **X-rays, MRIs, and CT scans**. This reduces clinician workload and speeds up diagnosis with greater accuracy.

- Automated analysis of medical images to suggest potential diagnostics
- Flagging of critical cases for faster physician review
- Providing confidence scores on detected conditions to guide decisions

Benefit of the Use Case

Improves **diagnostic accuracy, reduces clinician workload**, and **accelerates patient care**. Physicians and patients benefit through quicker and more reliable diagnostics.

Potential Risks by Implementing the Use Case

- Potential for false positives/negatives
- Over-reliance on AI recommendations by clinicians
- Data privacy and security issues

KPIs to Measure the Success of the Use Case

- Reduction in diagnostic time
- Increase in diagnostic accuracy rates

Data Requirements

- **Medical Imaging Data**: High-resolution images (X-rays, MRIs, CT scans)
- **Clinical Outcomes Data**: Historical diagnostic results to train models
- **Patient Metadata**: Age, health conditions, and case-specific information

Selected GenAI Taxonomy Dimensions

The following taxonomy, also introduced in Figure 4 - GenAI Use Case Taxonomy, classifies this Use Case along the relevant dimensions.

Taxonomy			
Business Dimension	Operational Efficiency	Customer Engagement	Products & Services
GenAI Capability	Language / Text	Media	Decision Support	Knowledge Discovery
Human Interaction	Advisory	Cooperative	Autonomous
Data Sensitvity	Public	Internal	Confidential	Secret

#10 Individualized Education Assistant

Business Dimension	Products & Services
Industry	Public (Education Sector)
Objective	Personalized assistance to optimize student learning pathways.

Usual Situation & Challenge

Many students face challenges in personalized learning due to **generic lesson plans** that fail to accommodate **different learning speeds and styles**. Teachers struggle to provide **customized attention** to all pupils, leading to **engagement gaps**.

GenAI Approach

An AI-driven assistant customizes learning experiences by **analyzing student performance** and providing tailored recommendations, feedback, and interactive content. Adaptive pathways improve engagement and outcomes.

- Personalizes study plans based on learning pace
- Provides instant explanations and practice questions
- Adapts teaching content based on progress and interests

Benefit of the Use Case

Students gain **enhanced comprehension and retention** due to tailored content delivery, while educators benefit from reduced workload and **improved classroom engagement**.

Potential Risks by Implementing the Use Case

- Privacy concerns with data use
- Potential biases in learning content
- High dependency on AI tools

KPIs to Measure the Success of the Use Case

- Improved student engagement and learning outcomes
- Reduction in educator workload for individualized plans

Data Requirements

- **Student performance data**: Grades, strengths, and weaknesses
- **Behavioral data**: Engagement levels, session duration
- **Curriculum data**: Syllabi, lesson plans, and educational standards

Selected GenAI Taxonomy Dimensions

The following taxonomy, also introduced in Figure 4 - GenAI Use Case Taxonomy, classifies this Use Case along the relevant dimensions.

Taxonomy				
Business Dimension	Operational Efficiency	Customer Engagement		Products & Services
GenAI Capability	Language / Text	Media	Decision Support	Knowledge Discovery
Human Interaction	Advisory	Cooperative		Autonomous
Data Sensitvity	Public	Internal	Confidential	Secret

10

of GenAI Use Cases for
Customer Engagement

#11 | Customer Sentiment Analysis

Business Dimension	Customer Engagement
Industry	Industry-Agnostic
Objective	Monitor and classify customer sentiment from feedback.

Usual Situation & Challenge

Financial institutions receive large volumes of unstructured customer feedback from multiple channels. **Identifying trends, dissatisfaction, or emerging issues** is time-consuming and often inconsistent when done manually.

GenAI Approach

Utilize GenAI models to analyze and classify customer sentiment across textual feedback from various channels, detecting emotional tone and key concerns automatically. **Advanced language processing capabilities** enable continuous monitoring and insight generation in real time.

- Sentiment categorization (positive, negative, neutral)
- Automated alerts for emerging sentiment trends
- Sentiment-driven customer service prioritization
- Integration with customer experience (CX) analytics

Benefit of the Use Case

Improves **customer satisfaction** and loyalty by enabling responsive engagement strategies. **Customer service teams benefit** by targeting areas of dissatisfaction and improving support efficiency.

Potential Risks by Implementing the Use Case

- Sentiment misclassification leading to biased insights
- Overreliance on AI interpretations
- Data privacy concerns in sensitive data processing

KPIs to Measure the Success of the Use Case

- Reduction in negative customer feedback response time
- Improvement in customer satisfaction scores

Data Requirements

- Text data from customer feedback channels (e.g., surveys, emails, chat logs)
- Historical sentiment analysis data to refine model accuracy
- Metadata for feedback categorization (e.g., demographics, issue type)

Selected GenAI Taxonomy Dimensions

The following taxonomy, also introduced in Figure 4 - GenAI Use Case Taxonomy, classifies this Use Case along the relevant dimensions.

Taxonomy			
Business Dimension	Operational Efficiency	Customer Engagement	Products & Services
GenAI Capability	Language / Text	Media	Decision Support	Knowledge Discovery
Human Interaction	Advisory	Cooperative	Autonomous
Data Sensitvity	Public	Internal	Confidential	Secret

#12 Intelligent Service Request Routing

Business Dimension	Customer Engagement
Industry	Industry-Agnostic
Objective	Optimized call routing to enhance user intent recognition.

Usual Situation & Challenge

Customer service centers often face **high call volumes** and **misrouted calls** due to manual routing based on limited data. This results in **longer response times**, poor service, and customer frustration.

GenAI Approach

Intelligent routing uses **GenAI-driven NLP models** to analyze and interpret caller intent from spoken or written requests. Calls are automatically routed to **appropriate departments** or personnel, minimizing errors and response times.

- Analyzes caller data and intent in real-time
- Improves accuracy of routing based on advanced language understanding
- Reduces reliance on human intervention in call sorting

Benefit of the Use Case

Enhanced **response speed and accuracy** lead to **better customer satisfaction** and **reduced operational costs**. Both customers and support staff benefit from more efficient query handling.

Potential Risks by Implementing the Use Case

- Inaccurate intent recognition leading to misrouting
- Data privacy issues when processing sensitive information
- Over-reliance on GenAI could cause disruptions if systems fail

KPIs to Measure the Success of the Use Case

- Call resolution time
- Call routing accuracy

Data Requirements

- **Caller Interaction Data:** Historical customer service calls for model training
- **Intent Classification Data:** Categorized user requests for refining routing logic
- **Departmental Response Data:** Performance metrics for different routing outcomes

Selected GenAI Taxonomy Dimensions

The following taxonomy, also introduced in Figure 4 - GenAI Use Case Taxonomy, classifies this Use Case along the relevant dimensions.

Taxonomy			
Business Dimension	Operational Efficiency	Customer Engagement	Products & Services
GenAI Capability	Language / Text	Media	Decision Support	Knowledge Discovery
Human Interaction	Advisory	Cooperative	Autonomous
Data Sensitvity	Public	Internal	Confidential	Secret

#13 | AI Health Chatbot

Business Dimension	Customer Engagement
Industry	Health
Objective	Personalized health guidance for patients via AI chatbot.

Usual Situation & Challenge

Patients often face **delays, generic advice**, and limited access to personalized healthcare, especially outside clinic hours. This can lead to **frustration, inadequate self-care**, and **misinformation**.

GenAI Approach

A conversational AI health chatbot leverages **natural language generation and decision support** capabilities to provide personalized healthcare advice, triage symptoms, and direct patients to relevant resources or professionals.

- 24/7 conversational support with personalized advice
- Adaptive responses based on patient history and preferences
- Symptom triage and guided recommendations for healthcare pathways

Benefit of the Use Case

Improves **patient satisfaction, self-care**, and reduces **burden on medical staff**. Patients receive accurate, relevant guidance, enhancing **engagement and outcomes**.

Potential Risks by Implementing the Use Case

- Potential for incorrect health recommendations
- Data privacy and security concerns
- Over-reliance on automated advice

KPIs to Measure the Success of the Use Case

- Reduction in patient wait times for health-related queries
- Patient satisfaction and engagement scores

Data Requirements

- **Patient demographic and health data**: Used for personalized advice and responses.
- **Symptom and condition data**: Supports accurate symptom triage and recommendations.
- **Healthcare provider data**: Directory to guide patients to relevant professionals or facilities.

Selected GenAI Taxonomy Dimensions

The following taxonomy, also introduced in Figure 4 - GenAI Use Case Taxonomy, classifies this Use Case along the relevant dimensions.

Taxonomy			
Business Dimension	Operational Efficiency	Customer Engagement	Products & Services
GenAI Capability	Language / Text	Media	Decision Support	Knowledge Discovery
Human Interaction	Advisory		Cooperative	Autonomous
Data Sensitvity	Public	Internal	Confidential	Secret

#14 Localized Customer Service Assistant

Business Dimension	Customer Engagement
Industry	Industry-Agnostic
Objective	Enhance customer support with multilingual query handling.

Usual Situation & Challenge

Many public service agencies face **language barriers** and struggle to provide effective support to diverse populations, leading to delayed responses and frustrated users due to a **lack of accurate translations** and human resource limitations.

GenAI Approach

A GenAI-powered assistant uses **advanced language generation and translation models** to automatically interpret, translate, and respond to customer queries across multiple languages while maintaining context and accuracy, ensuring faster and culturally appropriate communication.

- Real-time translation of text and speech for multilingual customer queries
- Context usage for culturally sensitive responses
- Seamless integration with existing customer workflows

Benefit of the Use Case

Improves **customer satisfaction** by reducing response times and enhancing service quality for non-native speakers, **support staff productivity** is increased due to automated responses.

Potential Risks by Implementing the Use Case

- Data privacy concerns for sensitive information
- Misinterpretation of complex or cultural nuances
- Dependence on consistent language model updates

KPIs to Measure the Success of the Use Case

- Customer satisfaction score improvement
- Reduction in average response time

Data Requirements

- Multilingual customer query logs for training and improvement
- Language preference and context metadata for personalized responses
- Feedback data on customer service interactions for model fine-tuning

Selected GenAI Taxonomy Dimensions

The following taxonomy, also introduced in Figure 4 - GenAI Use Case Taxonomy, classifies this Use Case along the relevant dimensions.

Taxonomy				
Business Dimension	Operational Efficiency	Customer Engagement		Products & Services
GenAI Capability	Language / Text	Media	Decision Support	Knowledge Discovery
Human Interaction	Advisory		Cooperative	Autonomous
Data Sensitvity	Public	Internal	Confidential	Secret

#15 Personalized Investment Insights

Business Dimension	Customer Engagement
Industry	Financial
Objective	Personalized investment recommendations for users.

Usual Situation & Challenge

Investors often face overwhelming market data, complex financial trends, and lack actionable, tailored insights. Manual financial planning limits personalization and scalability, leading to suboptimal investment strategies.

GenAI Approach

Generative AI analyzes individual investor data, market trends, and risk tolerance to generate tailored investment insights and strategies. Advanced language models provide actionable recommendations via user-friendly interfaces.

- Automated analysis of customer portfolios
- Real-time trend updates and predictive forecasting
- Personalized investment scenario simulations

Benefit of the Use Case

Investors receive highly personalized, actionable insights, improving decision-making and portfolio outcomes, while financial firms enhance customer satisfaction and retention.

Potential Risks by Implementing the Use Case

- Bias in recommendations
- Data security and privacy concerns
- Reliance on model accuracy

KPIs to Measure the Success of the Use Case

- Increase in customer portfolio performance
- Customer engagement metrics (e.g., time spent using insights)

Data Requirements

- **Customer financial data**: Historical transactions, portfolio composition, risk profile
- **Market data**: Stock trends, market sentiment, macroeconomic indicators
- **User engagement data**: Interaction history, preferences for insights

Selected GenAI Taxonomy Dimensions

The following taxonomy, also introduced in Figure 4 - GenAI Use Case Taxonomy, classifies this Use Case along the relevant dimensions.

Taxonomy				
Business Dimension	Operational Efficiency	Customer Engagement		Products & Services
GenAI Capability	Language / Text	Media	Decision Support	Knowledge Discovery
Human Interaction	Advisory	Cooperative		Autonomous
Data Sensitvity	Public	Internal	Confidential	Secret

#16 Virtual Product Specialist in Manufacturing

Business Dimension	Customer Engagement
Industry	Manufacturing
Objective	Enhance customer support by providing instant, in-depth product information.

Usual Situation & Challenge

Customers often struggle to understand complex products, leading to frustration and a lengthy support cycle. **Product specifications** and **technical details** can overwhelm, requiring **extensive human support**. Manufacturers need scalable solutions to communicate detailed, technical information clearly and accurately.

GenAI Approach

Leveraging GenAI's **language generation** capabilities. This AI-driven assistant responds to customer queries with precise, contextual product information and can adjust responses based on customer expertise levels.

- Offers **24/7 support** for instant customer assistance
- Uses **conversational AI** for a human-like experience
- Provides **detailed, accurate information** for complex technical inquiries

Benefit of the Use Case

Manufacturers benefit by **reducing human support costs** and improving **customer satisfaction**. Customers receive **accurate**

answers instantly, **streamlining decision-making** and minimizing the need for human intervention.

Potential Risks by Implementing the Use Case

- Misinterpretation of technical details
- Inadequate handling of complex, non-standard queries
- Dependence on accurate data input and maintenance

KPIs to Measure the Success of the Use Case

- Reduction in customer support requests requiring human agents
- Customer satisfaction scores on virtual support interactions

Data Requirements

- **Product Specifications**: Detailed technical data for each product
- Customer Interaction History: To personalize responses
- **Industry Standards and Compliance**: Ensuring information provided meets regulatory requirements

Selected GenAI Taxonomy Dimensions

The following taxonomy, also introduced in Figure 4 - GenAI Use Case Taxonomy, classifies this Use Case along the relevant dimensions.

	Taxonomy			
Business Dimension	Operational Efficiency	Customer Engagement		Products & Services
GenAI Capability	Language / Text	Media	Decision Support	Knowledge Discovery
Human Interaction	Advisory		Cooperative	Autonomous
Data Sensitvity	Public	Internal	Confidential	Secret

#17 | Customer Profile Enrichment

Business Dimension	Customer Engagement
Industry	Industry-Agnostic
Objective	Enrich customer profiles with real-time insights from behavioral data.

Usual Situation & Challenge

Customer profiles often lack in-depth behavioral insights, leading to **generic interactions** and **missed personalization opportunities**. **Behavioral data** is fragmented across multiple systems, making it challenging to derive a **holistic view** of each customer's preferences and behavior.

GenAI Approach

Using GenAI for **behavioral analysis and knowledge discovery**, customer profiles are enriched based on real-time activity data to generate **insightful, actionable attributes**. GenAI models identify behavioral patterns and update profiles accordingly.

- Automatically **classifies behaviors** into personalized tags
- **Predicts customer needs** based on previous actions and preferences
- Provides **real-time updates** for immediate targeting

Benefit of the Use Case

Improved **customer experience** and **increased engagement** as companies can personalize offers, recommendations, and communications based on a deep understanding of each customer's behavior, leading to **higher conversion rates**.

Potential Risks by Implementing the Use Case

- Privacy concerns around behavioral data tracking
- Data inaccuracies impacting personalization
- Potential over-reliance on AI-driven profiling for customer interactions

KPIs to Measure the Success of the Use Case

- Increase in personalized engagement metrics (e.g., click-through rate, response rate)
- **Reduction in churn rate** due to improved customer satisfaction

Data Requirements

- **Behavioral Data**: Interaction history, browsing, purchase, and response patterns
- **Demographic Data**: Age, location, interests, for contextual relevance
- **Transaction Data**: Purchase history to link behavior with spending trends

Selected GenAI Taxonomy Dimensions

The following taxonomy, also introduced in Figure 4 - GenAI Use Case Taxonomy, classifies this Use Case along the relevant dimensions.

Taxonomy				
Business Dimension	Operational Efficiency	Customer Engagement		Products & Services
GenAI Capability	Language / Text	Media	Decision Support	Knowledge Discovery
Human Interaction	Advisory		Cooperative	Autonomous
Data Sensitvity	Public	Internal	Confidential	Secret

#18 | Feedback-Driven Ad Creation

Business Dimension	Customer Engagement
Industry	Industry-Agnostic
Objective	Generate personalized ads using customer sentiment insights.

Usual Situation & Challenge

Traditional ads often fail to resonate due to generic messaging that doesn't align with customer sentiment. Creating ads that reflect real customer experiences requires significant time and resources, impacting engagement.

GenAI Approach

Leverage GenAI to analyze customer feedback and generate **targeted ad content** that aligns with customer sentiment. The AI assesses product reviews, social media feedback, and customer surveys to craft messaging that reflects real user sentiment.

- Analyzes **real-time feedback** for responsive ads
- Generates **dynamic ad content** for diverse customer groups
- Adjusts ad tone and style to **match customer sentiment**

Benefit of the Use Case

Businesses achieve **higher engagement** and **conversion rates** by aligning ad content with customer sentiment, leading to more **effective marketing** and **personalized customer experiences**.

Potential Risks by Implementing the Use Case

- Risk of over-personalizing and alienating segments
- Incorrect sentiment analysis leading to mismatched tone
- Data privacy concerns with customer feedback analysis

KPIs to Measure the Success of the Use Case

- **Increase in ad engagement rates** (e.g., click-through rates)
- Customer satisfaction scores on ad relevance

Data Requirements

- **Customer Sentiment Data**: From reviews, social media, and surveys
- **Historical Ad Performance**: For baseline comparisons and optimization
- **Customer Demographics**: To tailor ad content by segment

Selected GenAI Taxonomy Dimensions

The following taxonomy, also introduced in Figure 4 - GenAI Use Case Taxonomy, classifies this Use Case along the relevant dimensions.

Taxonomy				
Business Dimension	Operational Efficiency	Customer Engagement		Products & Services
GenAI Capability	Language / Text	Media	Decision Support	Knowledge Discovery
Human Interaction	Advisory	Cooperative		Autonomous
Data Sensitvity	Public	Internal	Confidential	Secret

#19 Automated Customer Survey Generation

Business Dimension	Customer Engagement
Industry	Industry-Agnostic
Objective	Generate highly personalized and relevant customer surveys efficiently.

Usual Situation & Challenge

Organizations often rely on **generic surveys** that do not consider **customer history** or **preferences**, leading to **low response rates** and **insufficient feedback**. Manually creating tailored surveys is **time-intensive** and lacks scalability.

GenAI Approach

Use GenAI's **language generation** to create **tailored surveys** based on customer profiles, interaction history, and preferences. The solution adapts survey content to improve relevance and engagement.

- **Personalizes** surveys for customer relevance
- **Automates** survey creation, reducing manual effort
- Adjusts **tone and complexity** based on customer segment

Benefit of the Use Case

By increasing **survey relevance**, response rates improve, enabling organizations to collect **meaningful insights**. **Marketing and customer service** teams benefit by understanding customer needs more precisely.

Potential Risks by Implementing the Use Case

- Risk of over-personalization leading to privacy concerns
- Data dependency: Needs accurate, updated customer data
- Survey fatigue: Frequent surveys may deter customers

KPIs to Measure the Success of the Use Case

- Survey response rate
- Quality and completeness of feedback

Data Requirements

- **Customer Profiles**: Demographics, preferences, purchase history
- **Interaction History**: Past engagements to gauge satisfaction
- **Survey Response Trends**: Insights into past response patterns to avoid fatigue

Selected GenAI Taxonomy Dimensions

The following taxonomy, also introduced in Figure 4 - GenAI Use Case Taxonomy, classifies this Use Case along the relevant dimensions.

Taxonomy			
Business Dimension	Operational Efficiency	Customer Engagement	Products & Services
GenAI Capability	Language / Text	Media	Decision Support	Knowledge Discovery
Human Interaction	Advisory	Cooperative	Autonomous
Data Sensitvity	Public	Internal	Confidential	Secret

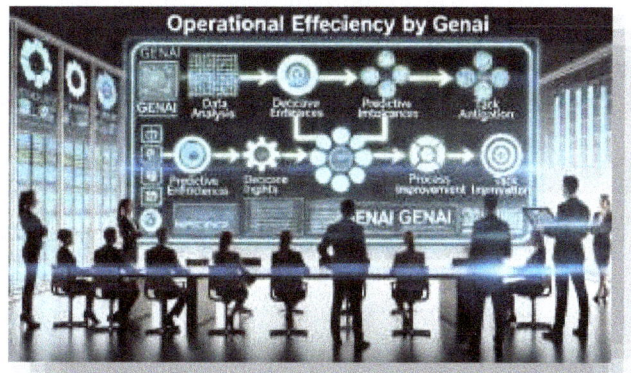

10

of GenAI Use Cases for
Operational Efficiency

#20 | Social Media Response Automation

Business Dimension	Customer Engagement
Industry	Public
Objective	Automate timely, relevant replies to social media inquiries and comments.

Usual Situation & Challenge

Public sector entities receive high volumes of questions and feedback on social media, which can overwhelm human teams and lead to **delays, inconsistency,** and **misinterpretation of inquiries**. Manual responses are **time-consuming** and increase the risk of **missed or misinformed replies.**

GenAI Approach

Deploy GenAI-driven **social media response automation** to analyze and respond accurately to public inquiries in real-time. AI models generate **contextual, consistent replies** aligned with public messaging, automating high-volume interactions while flagging sensitive cases for human follow-up.

- **Monitors** multiple channels in real-time
- **Generates responses** aligned with official information
- **Flags** sensitive topics for human review

Benefit of the Use Case

The public sector benefits by **improving responsiveness** and **reducing manual workload**, while citizens receive **timely,**

consistent responses that enhance trust and engagement with public services.

Potential Risks by Implementing the Use Case

- Potential for **misinterpretation** of sensitive topics
- Risk of **inadequate replies** in complex cases
- Public perception issues with AI-based responses

KPIs to Measure the Success of the Use Case

- **Response time** reduction for social media inquiries
- **User satisfaction** with social media interactions

Data Requirements

- **FAQ Database**: Predefined answers to frequently asked questions
- **Historical Interaction Data**: Previous responses and customer queries for AI training
- **Sentiment Analysis Data**: For understanding public sentiment and tonality adjustments

Selected GenAI Taxonomy Dimensions

The following taxonomy, also introduced in Figure 4 - GenAI Use Case Taxonomy, classifies this Use Case along the relevant dimensions.

Taxonomy				
Business Dimension	Operational Efficiency	Customer Engagement		Products & Services
GenAI Capability	Language / Text	Media	Decision Support	Knowledge Discovery
Human Interaction	Advisory	Cooperative		Autonomous
Data Sensitvity	Public	Internal	Confidential	Secret

#21 Financial Report Analysis Assistant

Business Dimension	Operational Efficiency (Finance)
Industry	Financial
Objective	Automate the analysis and summarization of complex financial reports.

Usual Situation & Challenge

Financial analysts spend extensive hours parsing through **large, complex reports**, which contain **critical financial insights** hidden in dense language and figures. Manual analysis is **time-consuming** and increases the risk of **human error**.

GenAI Approach

A **Financial Report Analysis Assistant** leverages GenAI's **language generation** and **knowledge discovery** capabilities to automate the extraction of key insights, trends, and summaries. It interprets financial data and generates concise reports with actionable recommendations.

- Summarizes lengthy reports in minutes
- Identifies key metrics and trends instantly
- **Automates routine analysis** for faster, more accurate insights

Benefit of the Use Case

Financial analysts and decision-makers benefit from **reduced time** spent on routine analysis and **improved accuracy** of insights, enabling them to **focus on strategic tasks** and decisions.

Potential Risks by Implementing the Use Case

- Misinterpretation of financial language nuances
- Over-reliance on AI-generated summaries
- Risk of data inaccuracies if not maintained

KPIs to Measure the Success of the Use Case

- Reduction in analysis time per financial report
- **Accuracy** of AI-generated summaries

Data Requirements

- **Financial Statements and Reports**: Core data for analysis (e.g., balance sheets, income statements)
- **Historical Financial Data**: To enable trend analysis and comparison
- **Regulatory Standards**: To ensure compliance in interpretations and recommendations

Selected GenAI Taxonomy Dimensions

The following taxonomy, also introduced in Figure 4 - GenAI Use Case Taxonomy, classifies this Use Case along the relevant dimensions.

Taxonomy				
Business Dimension	Operational Efficiency	Customer Engagement		Products & Services
GenAI Capability	Language / Text	Media	Decision Support	Knowledge Discovery
Human Interaction	Advisory	Cooperative		Autonomous
Data Sensitvity	Public	Internal	Confidential	Secret

#22 | Automated Literature Review

Business Dimension	Operational Efficiency (Research & Development)
Industry	Health, Manufacturing
Objective	Automate summarization of medical literature to speed up R&D.

Usual Situation & Challenge

R&D teams often spend **significant time** manually reviewing large volumes of scientific literature to identify relevant research insights. This process is **time-consuming** and **resource-intensive**, leading to **slower innovation cycles**.

GenAI Approach

Leverage GenAI for **automated literature reviews** by using **language generation** and **knowledge discovery** to summarize relevant findings from scientific publications. This streamlines information access for R&D teams, extracting key findings and trends.

- Automates literature summarization with high accuracy
- Prioritizes relevant studies based on R&D focus areas
- **Provides summarized insights** in natural language for easy interpretation

Benefit of the Use Case

Reduces **manual research time** and accelerates **R&D cycles**. R&D professionals benefit by accessing **concise summaries** that inform project direction and innovation opportunities, leading to **faster decision-making**.

Potential Risks by Implementing the Use Case

- Summarization errors due to ambiguous data
- Potential overlooking of critical research nuances
- High dependency on **updated** and **accurate datasets**

KPIs to Measure the Success of the Use Case

- **Reduction in time** spent on literature review
- **Increased speed** of R&D project completions

Data Requirements

- **Scientific Publications Database**: Full-text articles and metadata
- **Internal Research Records**: To provide contextual insights for filtering relevant information
- **Keywords and Topic Relevance Mapping**: Focus areas to guide GenAI model in prioritizing findings

Selected GenAI Taxonomy Dimensions

The following taxonomy, also introduced in Figure 4 - GenAI Use Case Taxonomy, classifies this Use Case along the relevant dimensions.

Taxonomy				
Business Dimension	Operational Efficiency	Customer Engagement		Products & Services
GenAI Capability	Language / Text	Media	Decision Support	Knowledge Discovery
Human Interaction	Advisory	Cooperative		Autonomous
Data Sensitvity	Public	Internal	Confidential	Secret

#23 Data Protection Audit Automation

Business Dimension	Operational Efficiency (Compliance)
Industry	Financial, Public
Objective	Automate audits to detect data protection gaps in compliance reports.

Usual Situation & Challenge

Data protection audits in finance are time-consuming, relying on **manual review** of extensive documents and reports, often missing **subtle compliance gaps** due to **high complexity** and **volume**. Ensuring complete compliance without errors is challenging and costly.

GenAI Approach

Use GenAI for **automated analysis** of compliance reports, identifying **data protection gaps** with advanced **language generation** and **knowledge discovery** capabilities. GenAI reviews large volumes of documents quickly and flags potential issues for human review.

- Automates identification of compliance issues
- Reduces time by streamlining report analysis
- Supports real-time compliance monitoring across systems

Benefit of the Use Case

Financial institutions gain **improved accuracy** and **speed in audits**, reducing human error and freeing up compliance teams to focus on strategic tasks. This boosts **regulatory adherence** while **minimizing costs**.

Potential Risks by Implementing the Use Case

- Missed identification of nuanced compliance gaps
- Potential over-reliance on AI, reducing manual oversight
- Data sensitivity concerns with automated processing

KPIs to Measure the Success of the Use Case

- Reduction in audit processing time
- Increase in compliance adherence rate

Data Requirements

- **Compliance Report Data**: Full-text compliance reports and audit documentation
- **Regulatory Standards**: Up-to-date data on legal and compliance regulations
- **Historical Audit Data**: Past audit results to refine and benchmark AI accuracy

Selected GenAI Taxonomy Dimensions

The following taxonomy, also introduced in Figure 4 - GenAI Use Case Taxonomy, classifies this Use Case along the relevant dimensions.

Taxonomy				
Business Dimension	Operational Efficiency	Customer Engagement		Products & Services
GenAI Capability	Language / Text	Media	Decision Support	Knowledge Discovery
Human Interaction	Advisory	Cooperative		Autonomous
Data Sensitvity	Public	Internal	Confidential	Secret

#24 Error Log Analysis & Summarization

Business Dimension	Operational Efficiency (IT)
Industry	Financial, Manufacturing
Objective	Summarize and categorize error logs for faster troubleshooting and resolution.

Usual Situation & Challenge

In many industries, error logs generate **huge amounts of unstructured data**, making it time-consuming and complex for IT teams to manually identify and categorize **recurring issues** and **root causes**. This often leads to prolonged **downtimes** and delays in **issue resolution**.

GenAI Approach

Leveraging GenAI for **error log analysis**, the solution automatically scans, categorizes, and summarizes error logs, identifying patterns and root causes. This reduces manual investigation and enables faster response.

- Automated log categorization for quick reference
- Summarization of error patterns to highlight critical issues
- **Root cause insights** for faster diagnosis

Benefit of the Use Case

IT and operational teams benefit from **faster troubleshooting** and **reduced downtime**. The automated summaries provide clear insights for prioritizing and addressing **recurring issues**, improving overall **system uptime**.

Potential Risks by Implementing the Use Case

- Misclassification of errors or patterns
- Incomplete coverage of complex error scenarios
- Dependency on the quality and accuracy of input logs

KPIs to Measure the Success of the Use Case

- Reduction in average resolution time for recurring issues
- **Decrease in system downtime** due to faster root cause identification

Data Requirements

- **Error Log Data**: Detailed error messages and timestamps for each log entry
- **Historical Incident Records**: Previous error and resolution records to recognize patterns
- **System Performance Data**: Context for the environment where the errors occurred

Selected GenAI Taxonomy Dimensions

The following taxonomy, also introduced in Figure 4 - GenAI Use Case Taxonomy, classifies this Use Case along the relevant dimensions.

Taxonomy				
Business Dimension	Operational Efficiency	Customer Engagement		Products & Services
GenAI Capability	Language / Text	Media	Decision Support	Knowledge Discovery
Human Interaction	Advisory		Cooperative	Autonomous
Data Sensitvity	Public	Internal	Confidential	Secret

#25 | Contract Terms Extraction

Business Dimension	Operational Efficiency (Contract Management)
Industry	Industry-Agnostic
Objective	Automate extraction of key terms from contracts for faster processing.

Usual Situation & Challenge

In high-volume contract environments, **manually reviewing contracts** to extract key terms such as **payment terms, liability clauses, and termination conditions** is labor-intensive and prone to **human error**. This leads to delays and inconsistencies in enforcing contract terms, affecting operational alignment.

GenAI Approach

Use **GenAI language generation and knowledge discovery** to extract and highlight key terms within contracts automatically. This system reads and parses complex documents, rapidly identifying critical terms for further review or integration into management systems.

- **Automates extraction** of predefined key terms
- **Reduces manual work** and improves accuracy
- Enables **fast processing** and **real-time contract compliance checks**

Benefit of the Use Case

Both financial and manufacturing teams benefit from **reduced processing time** and **improved contract accuracy**, leading to

better compliance and **faster onboarding** of contractual obligations.

Potential Risks by Implementing the Use Case

- Misinterpretation of nuanced contractual language
- Dependence on highly accurate and up-to-date contract
- Potential data security concerns with contract data

KPIs to Measure the Success of the Use Case

- **Reduction in time spent** on contract processing
- **Improvement in accuracy** of term extraction and compliance rates

Data Requirements

- **Contract Templates**: Standardized language for terms
- **Historical Contract Data**: To train the model on specific clause structures
- **Compliance Requirements**: Key terms for contract adherence and legal conformity

Selected GenAI Taxonomy Dimensions

The following taxonomy, also introduced in Figure 4 - GenAI Use Case Taxonomy, classifies this Use Case along the relevant dimensions.

Taxonomy						
Business Dimension	Operational Efficiency		Customer Engagement		Products & Services	
GenAI Capability	Language / Text	Media		Decision Support	Knowledge Discovery	
Human Interaction	Advisory		Cooperative		Autonomous	
Data Sensitvity	Public		Internal	Confidential		Secret

#26 Code Completion & Suggestion Tool

Business Dimension	Operational Efficiency (IT)
Industry	Industry-agnostic
Objective	Provide intelligent code suggestions to boost development speed and accuracy.

Usual Situation & Challenge

Developers often face productivity bottlenecks, spending significant time on **routine coding tasks**, troubleshooting syntax, or recalling best practices. These issues **delay projects** and can lead to **inconsistent code quality**.

GenAI Approach

Implement a **code completion and suggestion tool** using **language generation** capabilities. This GenAI-powered assistant predicts and suggests code snippets, optimizes syntax, and follows coding best practices to aid developers.

1. Provides **real-time code suggestions** for faster coding
2. **Autocompletes complex code** based on context and previous patterns
3. Reduces **syntax errors** and ensures code consistency

Benefit of the Use Case

Developers benefit from **increased productivity** and **reduced debugging time**, enabling faster project completion with **improved code quality**. Companies experience **reduced**

development costs and more consistent **software delivery timelines**.

Potential Risks by Implementing the Use Case

- Risk of incorrect code suggestions
- Dependence on tool accuracy, impacting critical code decisions
- Potential data security risks if proprietary code is exposed

KPIs to Measure the Success of the Use Case

- Reduction in coding time per task or project
- Decrease in syntax errors and code inconsistencies

Data Requirements

- **Existing Codebase**: To learn patterns and context-specific recommendations
- **Coding Standards & Best Practices**: For consistent quality and adherence to guidelines
- **User Feedback on Suggestions**: To continuously improve the tool's accuracy

Selected GenAI Taxonomy Dimensions

The following taxonomy, also introduced in Figure 4 - GenAI Use Case Taxonomy, classifies this Use Case along the relevant dimensions.

	Taxonomy			
Business Dimension	Operational Efficiency	Customer Engagement		Products & Services
GenAI Capability	Language / Text	Media	Decision Support	Knowledge Discovery
Human Interaction	Advisory	Cooperative		Autonomous
Data Sensitvity	Public	Internal	Confidential	Secret

#27 | Invoice Assistant

Business Dimension	Operational Efficiency (Invoice Processing and Categorization)
Industry	Industry-Agnostic
Objective	Automate and streamline invoice categorization by department.

Usual Situation & Challenge

Manual invoice categorization is **time-consuming, error-prone**, and often requires cross-departmental effort for validation. This delays financial processing and introduces inaccuracies.

GenAI Approach

Using GenAI, an intelligent assistant **automatically classifies invoices** by analyzing content, identifying relevant metadata, and cross-referencing with department information. Reduces errors, accelerates invoice handling, and integrates seamlessly with existing ERP systems.

- NLP models extract key data points from invoices (e.g., vendor, amount, department codes)
- Real-time categorization using pre-trained models tailored to industry-specific needs
- Continuous learning and optimization based on user feedback

Benefit of the Use Case

Faster processing times, reduced errors, and **enhanced compliance** for accounts payable teams. **Departments benefit from improved resource allocation** and streamlined workflows.

Potential Risks by Implementing the Use Case

- Data privacy issues if handling confidential information
- Misclassification of invoices in edge cases
- Resistance to change from manual processes

KPIs to Measure the Success of the Use Case

- Reduction in invoice processing time
- Reduction in invoice categorization errors

Data Requirements

- Historical invoice data (e.g., past categorizations, formats)
- Metadata of departments and vendors (for accurate classification)
- Invoice content (structured and unstructured text)

Selected GenAI Taxonomy Dimensions

The following taxonomy, also introduced in Figure 4 - GenAI Use Case Taxonomy, classifies this Use Case along the relevant dimensions.

Taxonomy				
Business Dimension	Operational Efficiency	Customer Engagement		Products & Services
GenAI Capability	Language / Text	Media	Decision Support	Knowledge Discovery
Human Interaction	Advisory	Cooperative		Autonomous
Data Sensitvity	Public	Internal	Confidential	Secret

#28 | Automatic Meeting Transcript Generator

Business Dimension	Operational Efficiency (Administrative Productivity)
Industry	Industry-Agnostic
Objective	Automatically transcribe and summarize meetings for streamlined information sharing.

Usual Situation & Challenge

Teams often spend significant time manually taking notes, risking **loss of important details** and **inconsistent summaries**. This inefficiency can lead to **miscommunication** and **repeated clarifications** in follow-up meetings also when details are missed.

GenAI Approach

Deploy a GenAI-powered **Automatic Meeting Transcript Generator** that listens to meetings in real-time and generates **summarized transcripts** with key action points, decisions, and highlights. This summary is easily shareable with others.

- **Real-time transcription** of spoken language into text
- **Summarizes key takeaways** and action items
- **Reduces need for manual note-taking** and post-meeting documentation

Benefit of the Use Case

Teams benefit from **enhanced productivity**, as information is quickly accessible and **decision-making** is streamlined.

Summaries ensure **consistency** and **easy follow-ups** across teams, reducing administrative burden.

Potential Risks by Implementing the Use Case

- Accuracy issues with technical terms or jargon
- Potential privacy concerns in recorded meetings
- Dependence on high-quality audio for transcription

KPIs to Measure the Success of the Use Case

- Reduction in time spent on manual note-taking
- Improvement in post-meeting clarity and follow-through on action items

Data Requirements

- **Audio Recordings of Meetings**: High-quality audio for transcription accuracy
- **Company Terminology Database**: Ensure accurate transcription of industry-specific terms
- **Participant Information**: To label and attribute comments in the transcript

Selected GenAI Taxonomy Dimensions

The following taxonomy, also introduced in Figure 4 - GenAI Use Case Taxonomy, classifies this Use Case along the relevant dimensions.

Taxonomy				
Business Dimension	Operational Efficiency	Customer Engagement		Products & Services
GenAI Capability	Language / Text	Media	Decision Support	Knowledge Discovery
Human Interaction	Advisory	Cooperative		Autonomous
Data Sensitvity	Public	Internal	Confidential	Secret

#29 Internal Chatbot Knowledge Base

Business Dimension	Operational Efficiency (Workplace Productivity)
Industry	Industry-Agnostic
Objective	Quick access to internal knowledge for employee queries

Usual Situation & Challenge

Employees spend **significant time searching for information** across disparate systems, leading to delays in decision-making and reduced productivity, particularly for common or complex queries.

GenAI Approach

Leverage a **conversational chatbot** powered by Generative AI, trained on internal documents, policies, and FAQs to deliver accurate responses. The chatbot continuously learns from new data and employee interactions to improve query resolution.

- Fast and accurate retrieval of internal data
- Continuous learning and updates to knowledge base
- Reduced manual intervention for standard queries

Benefit of the Use Case

Increases employee productivity by providing instant answers, reducing information search time and improving overall operational efficiency. **HR, IT, and all employees** benefit by having consistent and rapid responses.

Potential Risks by Implementing the Use Case

- Data security and access control issues
- Potential for outdated responses if not updated
- Resistance to chatbot adoption

KPIs to Measure the Success of the Use Case

- Reduction in average query response time
- Employee satisfaction with chatbot responses

Data Requirements

- **Internal knowledge base** documents, including policies and FAQs
- **User query data** for training and refining responses
- **Feedback data** from users for continuous learning and improvement

Selected GenAI Taxonomy Dimensions

The following taxonomy, also introduced in Figure 4 - GenAI Use Case Taxonomy, classifies this Use Case along the relevant dimensions.

Taxonomy				
Business Dimension	Operational Efficiency	Customer Engagement		Products & Services
GenAI Capability	Language / Text	Media	Decision Support	Knowledge Discovery
Human Interaction	Advisory	Cooperative		Autonomous
Data Sensitvity	Public	Internal	Confidential	Secret

#30 | Technical Documentation Creation and Management

Business Dimension	Operational Efficiency (Knowledge Management & Process Optimization)
Industry	Financial, Manufacturing
Objective	Streamline documentation processes using GenAI capabilities

Usual Situation & Challenge

Creating, updating, and managing technical documentation is **time-consuming, prone to errors, and lacks consistency** across teams. This leads to inefficiencies, reduced operational clarity, and missed compliance requirements.

GenAI Approach

Leverage GenAI to **automate content generation, extract insights, and summarize updates** with consistent formatting and language precision. This involves creating drafts, maintaining document standards, and updating content from data changes.

- Automated content creation based on structured data
- Summarization and analysis of updates from regulatory changes
- Formatting and style standardization for consistency

Benefit of the Use Case

Improved **documentation accuracy, speed, and reduced manual effort** allow teams to focus on higher-value tasks. **Operational teams benefit** through faster updates and fewer errors in knowledge resources.

Potential Risks by Implementing the Use Case

- Inaccurate information generated by AI
- Risk of over-reliance on automation without human oversight
- Data security vulnerabilities

KPIs to Measure the Success of the Use Case

- Time reduction in document creation and updates
- Error rate in technical documentation

Data Requirements

- Historical documentation and previous content versions for context learning
- Regulatory updates and guidelines for compliance-driven changes
- Structured data sources from internal systems for accurate content generation

Selected GenAI Taxonomy Dimensions

The following taxonomy, also introduced in Figure 4 - GenAI Use Case Taxonomy, classifies this Use Case along the relevant dimensions.

Taxonomy				
Business Dimension	Operational Efficiency	Customer Engagement		Products & Services
GenAI Capability	Language / Text	Media	Decision Support	Knowledge Discovery
Human Interaction	Advisory	Cooperative		Autonomous
Data Sensitvity	Public	Internal	Confidential	Secret

How to Start With GenAI Use Cases

In today's rapidly advancing technological landscape, preparing for GenAI (Generative AI) is essential for organizations aiming to leverage AI-driven innovation effectively.

Before organizations can implement or scale GenAI use cases, foundational preparations are essential. To address this, we introduce a two-phase approach to initiate GenAI effectively, see Figure 6.

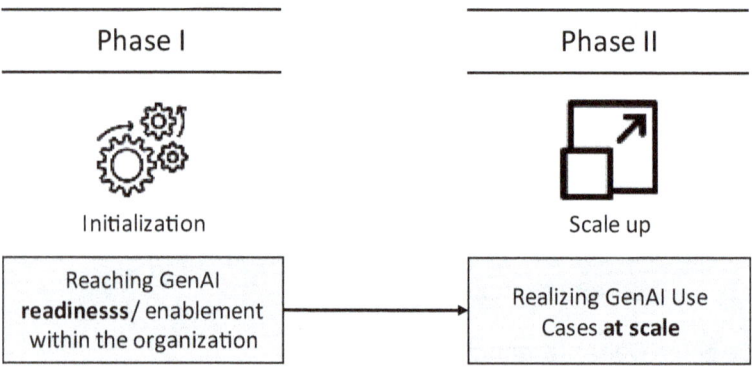

Figure 6 - Starting with GenAI

First, **GenAI readiness** must be achieved. This involves setting up necessary capabilities, aligning stakeholders, clarifying technology and compliance requirements, and securing management buy-in. Once readiness is established, organizations can then move to **ideate, develop, and scale GenAI use cases** in a standardized, structured manner that ensures long-term impact and integration across the organization.

Phase I – Initialization

Reaching GenAI readiness provides the foundation for sustainable, organization-wide GenAI deployment, ensuring that resources, infrastructure, and processes are aligned for long-term success. All starts with a structured procedure to introduce GenAI, see Figure 7. This process details the critical steps to establish GenAI readiness, a prerequisite before scaling up with broader GenAI use cases. Each phase builds the technical, operational, and strategic groundwork necessary to unlock GenAI's full potential.

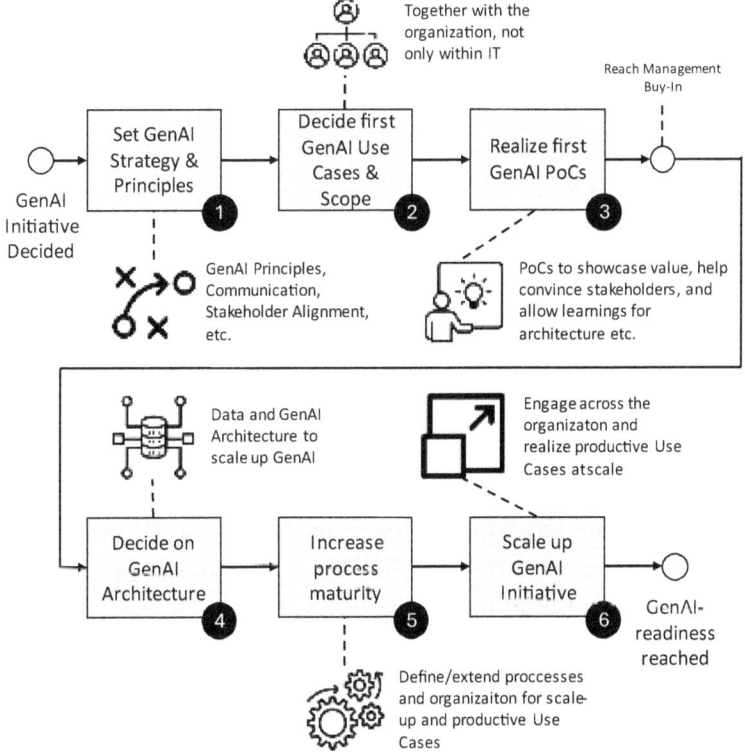

Figure 7 - How to achieve GenAI-readiness for the organization

The GenAI initiative begins with an overall commitment to **start the GenAI initiative**, where the organization formally commits to exploring GenAI's potential and outlines clear objectives aligned with its strategic goals. This initial status sets the direction and purpose for the GenAI journey.

1. Following this, **defining a GenAI strategy and establishing principles** is crucial. Here, foundational principles are set, such as beginning with a lean approach, prioritizing standardization, and preparing for scalability. These principles act as guiding rules that maintain focus and alignment across teams as the initiative progresses, ensuring decisions remain consistent with the organization's long-term objectives.

2. Next, it is essential to **decide initial GenAI use cases and scope**. Through collaboration with different business units, the organization identifies promising GenAI use cases that can demonstrate early value. These cases, often "low-hanging fruit" that are simple yet impactful, are chosen to establish quick wins. Aligning with stakeholders across departments ensures these use cases meet broader business needs and have organization-wide support, fostering a culture of acceptance and collaboration. The goal is to implement initial use cases on a lean scale that still deliver value, allowing the organization to see tangible results. **These early successes are crucial for gaining buy-in and ultimately achieving GenAI readiness** across the organization.

3. Once initial use cases are chosen, the organization moves to **execute the first GenAI proof of concepts (PoCs)**. These PoCs validate the feasibility and effectiveness of GenAI applications, providing tangible demonstrations of their potential. Successful PoCs not only showcase early value but also generate momentum, engaging and securing buy-in from key stakeholders, such as management and works councils, while addressing any concerns related to costs or organizational impacts.

Interim milestone: Securing **management buy-in** is a pivotal milestone. At this stage, with early successes and demonstrated value from PoCs, management's commitment is secured for further investments and resources. This milestone provides the official support needed to advance the GenAI initiative with the resources required for scaling.

4. Following management approval, the organization **establishes a GenAI architecture**. Based on insights and technical learnings from the PoCs, the organization identifies the necessary tools, infrastructure, and architecture for broader GenAI deployment. This architecture will support scalable operations, ensuring compatibility with the organization's strategic needs and technological capabilities.

5. To scale GenAI effectively, organizations need **an increased process maturity** to ensure efficient, compliant, and strategic development of GenAI Use Cases. This phase involves standardizing GenAI Use Case steps – from ideation to deployment – and ensuring compliance with data regulations like GDPR. Key roles are defined to support these processes: the Use Case Owner oversees project alignment with business goals; the Data Owner manages data quality, accessibility, and regulatory compliance; Compliance Teams address legal and privacy requirements; and IT, Security Teams, and End Users support infrastructure, security, and usability. Together, these roles and structured processes enable focused prioritization, directing resources toward high-value initiatives and providing a stable, compliant foundation for scaling GenAI across the organization.

6. Finally, with these structures in place, the organization can **scale up the GenAI initiative**. This phase involves opening communication channels for cross-departmental collaboration and systematically capturing ideas across functions. With both budget and infrastructure ready, the organization is positioned to meet increasing demand for GenAI applications efficiently and at scale.

Finally, achieving **GenAI readiness** marks the successful completion of this initiative. The organization now has a mature foundation for GenAI, equipped to scale use cases productively and reliably, setting the stage for transformative AI-driven growth across the enterprise.

Phase II – GenAI at Scale

With GenAI readiness established, Phase II focuses on scaling GenAI use cases across the organization. This phase moves from isolated projects to the broad integration of GenAI, enabling enterprise-wide impact. Building on initial successes and insights, organizations expand their GenAI portfolio, applying standardized processes and leveraging roles established in Phase.

The **Use Case Funnel** is part of the organizational initialization and increases the maturity of the processes for realizing GenAI Use Cases at scale, see Figure 8. It acts as a blueprint for achieving increased process maturity, providing a structured pathway for developing GenAI use cases from ideation through prioritization, PoC validation, and scaling. While it standardizes the journey from concept to deployment, it is flexible and needs to be adapted to fit each organization's unique needs, goals, and regulatory environment. Tailoring this process ensures that GenAI initiatives align with specific business priorities and deliver maximum value, driving consistent, compliant, and impactful adoption across the enterprise.

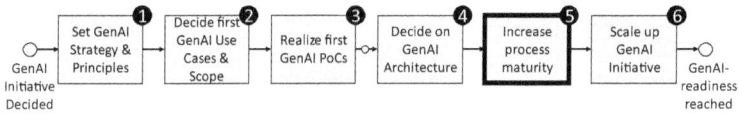

Figure 8 - Focusing on Process Maturity

The **Use Case Funnel**, as shown in Figure 9, is a structured process that guides organizations through identifying, validating, and scaling GenAI use cases effectively.

It moves from broad idea generation to focused prioritization, rigorous testing through Proof of Concepts (PoCs), iterative improvements, and finally, broad deployment. This funnel ensures that only the most valuable, feasible, and impactful GenAI initiatives are scaled, maximizing their business value while minimizing risk and resource waste.

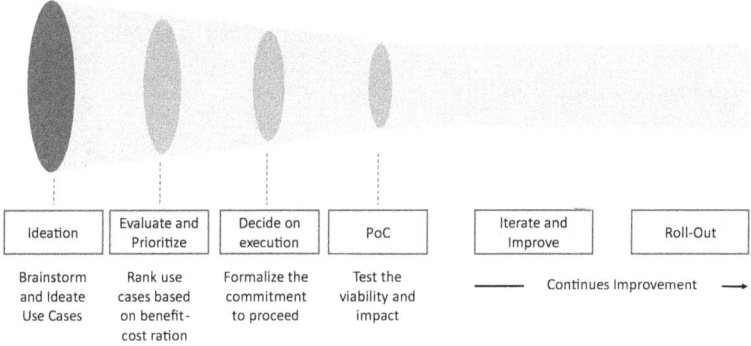

Figure 9 - GenAI Use Case Funnel

Ideation

This step focuses on generating potential GenAI use cases by engaging diverse business units to identify opportunities aligned with strategic goals. By capturing a wide range of ideas, it fosters innovation and ensures that valuable and relevant use cases are considered. This broad input helps align GenAI initiatives with real business challenges, laying a strong foundation for impactful projects.

Evaluate and Prioritize

Use cases are assessed based on their potential impact, feasibility, benefit-cost ratio, and alignment with strategic business objectives. This evaluation helps identify high-value, low-risk opportunities and ensures that resources are concentrated on the most promising initiatives. Effective prioritization maximizes early success and drives focus toward initiatives with tangible business outcomes.

Decide on Execution

This step formalizes the commitment to proceed with selected use cases by allocating resources, defining roles, and setting clear objectives for implementation. Establishing accountability, budgets, and timelines ensures that the project is ready for execution. This phase is critical for moving from planning to tangible action, creating a strong foundation for success.

Proof of Concept (PoC)

The PoC phase tests the feasibility, value, and impact of the selected GenAI use cases in a controlled setting. It validates assumptions, gathers feedback, and demonstrates tangible value while minimizing risks. Successful PoCs provide proof of value, engage stakeholders, and inform refinements for broader deployment.

Iterate and Improve

Based on feedback and results from the PoC, this phase focuses on refining and optimizing the use case to address gaps, enhance functionality, and better align with business needs. Continuous improvement ensures robust solutions capable of delivering sustained value. Iteration creates a stronger, more effective GenAI implementation.

Roll-Out

Successful use cases are expanded across departments with established processes, governance, and infrastructure. Cross-departmental collaboration ensures efficient deployment at scale, maximizing impact. Rolling out GenAI solutions enterprise-wide drives consistent value and accelerates digital transformation.

Use Case Selection to Build Maturity

This chapter focuses on identifying and scoping initial GenAI use cases that demonstrate early value and serve as "quick wins." By collaborating across business units and aligning with stakeholders, organizations can foster support and ensure use cases address broader needs. Lean-scale implementation of these impactful projects delivers quick results, builds momentum, and paves the way for broader GenAI adoption and readiness.

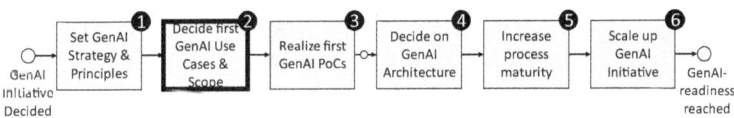

Figure 10 - Focusing on Deciding First GenAI Use Cases

Selecting the right initial use cases is crucial for showcasing the success and feasibility of GenAI. This ties back to Activity 2 in Phase I to achieve GenAI readiness, see Figure 10. The Benefit-Cost-Ratio (BCR) framework offers a strategic method to assess and prioritize GenAI use cases based on expected benefits and costs, considering both risk and implementation effort. It helps identify "low-hanging fruit" – use cases with significant impact and minimal risk – while aligning with organizational goals and resource constraints. This approach ensures that early GenAI projects are viable and impactful, laying a strong foundation for future success.

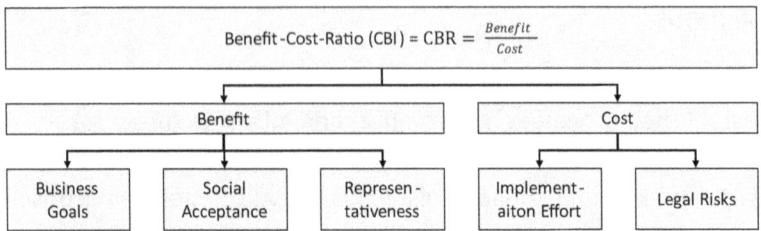

Figure 11 - Benefit-Cost-Reatio for Use Case Selection

The **BCR framework** is adaptable, allowing organizations to customize it to fit their strategic needs, regulatory environments, unique business goals, and specific enterprise needs. It is recommended to tailor the framework to enterprise needs to maximize relevance and impact. This flexibility ensures that the approach aligns with priorities and industry standards, leading to meaningful, actionable outcomes.

Key Components of the Benefit-Cost-Ratio Framework

The BCR framework assesses two primary components: Benefit and Cost.

Benefit

The Benefit component evaluates how each GenAI use case aligns with strategic objectives, stakeholder expectations, and potential scalability. This ensures selected use cases deliver immediate value and support future GenAI initiatives.

- **Business Goals Alignment**: Measures how well the use case supports critical business objectives. Each use case is rated on a scale of 0 to 5, with higher ratings reflecting stronger alignment with goals like revenue growth, customer experience, or operational efficiency.
- **Social Acceptance**: Assesses the level of internal support for the use case. High social acceptance drives smoother implementation and adoption. The rating (0-5) indicates how well the use case resonates with departments and stakeholders. This is also crucial for effective stakeholder

management, as lack of support can create resistance within the organization. Awareness should be given to whether certain stakeholders might not benefit or could even be negatively impacted by GenAI use cases, as this could lead to active opposition, including from works councils.
- **Representativeness**: Evaluates whether the use case can serve as a model for others in terms of technology, legal considerations, or process improvements. Highly representative use cases facilitate cross-functional learning and streamline future projects. Ratings (0-5) reflect their potential as scalable proof-of-concepts.

Cost

The Cost component focuses on obstacles, such as implementation effort and regulatory risks, helping organizations avoid resource-intensive projects that could delay results.

- **Implementation Effort**: Evaluates the time, resources, and technical complexity required. Lower-cost use cases are prioritized for faster results and reduced barriers to adoption. This evaluation can be done using a 0-5 rating or even by using story points, which are well-established in the software industry.
- **Legal and Compliance Risk**: Examines regulatory challenges, especially regarding laws like GDPR or the EU AI Act. High-risk use cases could face delays or additional compliance costs, making them less suitable as initial projects.

Use cases are assessed on these criteria, with a weighted score that allows for ranking by BCR. The highest-scoring cases are prioritized for their balanced combination of high benefits and manageable costs.

Importance of the BCR Framework

The BCR framework offers multiple benefits for an organization's GenAI adoption journey:

- **Identifying Quick Wins**: The methodology identifies low-cost, high-impact use cases that can quickly demonstrate GenAI's value, helping secure leadership and stakeholder support.
- **Mitigating Risks**: Evaluating costs and regulatory risks reduces the likelihood of unexpected obstacles, improving the chances of successful implementation.
- **Building Organizational Readiness**: Structured assessments foster collaboration across departments, ensuring buy-in and accelerating GenAI adoption, thereby fostering a culture of innovation.
- **Establishing a Foundation for Future Initiatives**: By focusing on representative use cases, organizations can develop insights and best practices to guide future GenAI projects, encouraging sustainable growth.

The Benefit-Cost-Ratio framework enables organizations to strategically select GenAI use cases that align with business goals, balance risks, and establish a foundation for scaling GenAI initiatives. These "low-hanging fruits" become quick wins, providing early, tangible results and helping companies to start securely with GenAI, making the initiative more successful and sustainable.

Example Based on 30 Presented Use Cases

Given the 30 use cases presented in this book, a short case study is presented. Then, use cases that do not fit the case study or industry are excluded. The remaining use cases are evaluated as examples for the case study, with specific weights for the criteria within cost and benefit chosen to reflect specific enterprise needs. Finally, the use cases are evaluated and sorted according to the BCR.

Example: A mid-sized manufacturing company specializing in industrial equipment faces increased pressure to innovate and remain competitive in an evolving industry. With no current GenAI implementations, the company recognizes the need to integrate GenAI to optimize their operations and enhance customer experience. Leadership understands that GenAI can be a key differentiator, especially in areas like predictive maintenance, quality control, and process automation. However, it still needs to be introduced and made available to the entire organization, which presents a significant challenge, as ensuring company-wide awareness and buy-in is crucial to avoid resistance.

Given the use cases presented, five have been decided for the proof of concept (PoC). In real companies, more use cases might be selected, but for this example, five are enough to illustrate the concept:

The following use cases from the list above, with their original numbers, are best suited to the example manufacturing company:

- Real-Time Equipment Health Monitoring (Use Case #1)
- Visual Inventory Management System (Use Case #5)
- Customer Sentiment Analysis (Use Case #11)
- Intelligent Service Request Routing (Use Case #12)
- Error Log Analysis & Summarization (Use Case #25)

The above-mentioned criteria are reused in the table to illustrate their applicability, with abbreviations used for better readability. BG is for Business Goals, SA for Social Acceptance, RE for Representativeness, IE for Implementation Effort, and LR for Legal Risk. The weighted sum for Benefit (B) is calculated as follows: BG is weighted with 0.4, SA with 0.4, and RE with 0.2.

For Cost (C), IE and LR are each weighted with 0.5. The weighted sum is obtained by multiplying each criterion's value by its respective weight and summing them up. These weights are used for calculating the weighted sums for B and C, but they should be adjusted according to enterprise needs. BCR (Benefit-Cost-Ratio) is then calculated as B divided by C.

Use Case #	Benefit				Cost			BCR
	BG	SA	RE	B	IE	LR	C	
Use Case #1	3	4	5	3,9	3	2	2,5	1,52
Use Case #5	4	3	4	3,6	3	1	2,0	1,80
Use Case #11	4	5	3	4,2	2	2	2,0	2,10
Use Case #12	4	4	4	4,0	3	1	2,0	2,00
Use Case #25	2	3	4	3,0	3	1	2,0	1,40

Based on the evaluation, Use Case #11 has the highest BCR (2.10) and was selected as the starting point for implementation due to its strong benefit-cost balance.

Further criteria might be added depending on specific enterprise situations, and the weights used for the calculations likely need to be adjusted to reflect the unique needs of each enterprise. Additionally, multiple use cases can be selected simultaneously to support good architectural decisions and ensure a more comprehensive implementation approach.

Legal and Ethical Concerns

Artificial Intelligence (AI) has rapidly evolved into a transformative technology, offering benefits and opportunities across numerous fields. However, alongside these opportunities, the integration of AI also brings significant legal and ethical concerns that need careful consideration. This chapter aims to explore these issues, focusing on the ethical and regulatory landscape surrounding the use of AI. Specifically, we will delve into the risks related to fairness, explainability, privacy, intellectual property, artificial hallucination, and the broader organizational impact.

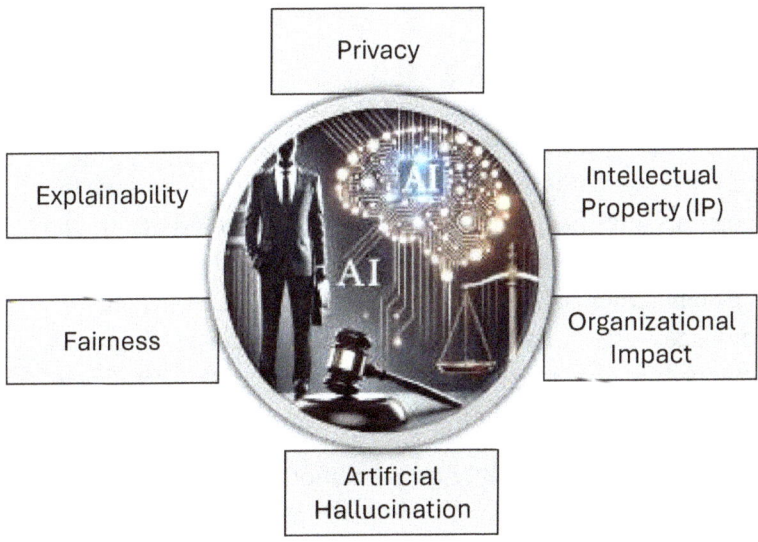

Figure 12 - Legal and Ethical Concerns

Fairness is a fundamental concern because AI systems can unintentionally perpetuate or even exacerbate biases. For instance, if an AI model used for hiring is trained on historical data that reflects past discriminatory hiring practices, it may continue to favor certain demographics over others. This leads to unfair treatment, where qualified candidates from underrepresented groups may be overlooked simply because the data used to train the AI contains inherent biases. Ensuring fairness requires constant evaluation and updating of training data to mitigate such biases and strive for equitable outcomes.

Explainability presents another critical issue. Many AI models, especially those based on deep learning, function as "black boxes," meaning their decision-making processes are opaque and difficult to interpret. For example, a financial institution using an AI system to approve or reject loan applications may find it challenging to explain why certain individuals were denied loans. This lack of transparency can undermine trust, especially when customers demand clear reasons for such important decisions. Creating more interpretable AI models or providing tools to better understand their reasoning is essential to address this concern.

Privacy concerns revolve around the collection and usage of user data, often without sufficient consent or awareness. AI systems rely on large datasets for training, which may include sensitive personal information. For example, an AI-powered health app might collect and store users' medical data without fully informing them of how this information will be used. Such practices raise ethical questions about user consent and data ownership. Additionally, improper handling of this data could lead to breaches, compromising users' privacy and security.

Intellectual Property (IP) rights are another area of concern, as questions arise regarding the ownership of AI-generated content and derived insights. For instance, if an AI system generates a new piece of music, who holds the copyright – the developer of the AI, the user who provided the input, or the AI itself? Similarly, if an AI model is trained on proprietary data without permission, it may lead to IP infringement. Resolving these issues requires clear legal frameworks that define ownership and usage rights for AI-generated content.

Artificial hallucination refers to instances where AI generates misleading or entirely incorrect information. This can be particularly problematic in critical applications. For example, if an AI system used in healthcare suggests an incorrect diagnosis based on patient data, it could lead to inappropriate treatment and potential harm. These hallucinations occur because AI models may generate responses based on patterns they have learned, even when those patterns do not apply to the specific context. Ensuring that AI systems are rigorously tested and validated is crucial to minimize such risks.

The **organizational impact** of AI should also be considered carefully. Incorrect AI outputs can lead to a loss of trust among stakeholders. For example, if an AI system used in customer service consistently provides incorrect or unhelpful answers, customers may lose confidence in the company's ability to address their needs. Additionally, integrating AI into existing workflows can be challenging, as it often requires changes in processes and employee roles. Organizations may face resistance from staff who are concerned about job displacement or who struggle to adapt to new AI-driven tools. To address these challenges, it is important to focus on change management, employee training, and maintaining transparency about how AI will be used.

Introducing generative AI (GenAI) offers many opportunities, but it is essential to consider these legal and ethical aspects to protect individuals and increase acceptance. Without addressing these concerns, any GenAI initiative is likely to fail, as neglecting them could lead to biases, privacy violations, loss of trust, and ultimately, the rejection of the technology by both users and stakeholders.

Shaping the Future with GenAI

As organizations achieve GenAI readiness and scale their initiatives, the potential for transformative growth and innovation is immense. The GenAI landscape is rapidly evolving, promising breakthroughs in automation, creativity, and decision-making capabilities. Businesses that strategically integrate GenAI will lead their industries, pioneering customer experiences, operational efficiencies, and new market opportunities. However, the journey doesn't end with implementation; it requires continuous adaptation, learning, and strategic foresight.

Looking ahead, companies must be prepared to navigate challenges such as evolving regulations, ethical AI considerations, and competitive pressures. Staying ahead will demand a commitment to innovation, robust data governance, and fostering a culture of experimentation and collaboration. The ability to scale GenAI responsibly and ethically will differentiate true leaders from followers in the digital economy.

This book has provided a structured roadmap for achieving GenAI success – from identifying and prioritizing impactful use cases to building scalable and compliant AI solutions. As you move forward, consider GenAI as a cornerstone of your digital strategy, driving meaningful outcomes and setting the stage for sustained competitive advantage. By staying agile, fostering innovation, and continuously refining your approach, you can turn the promise of GenAI into a lasting reality for your organization and its customers. Embrace the future of GenAI; the possibilities are limitless.

www.ingramcontent.com/pod-product-compliance
Lightning Source LLC
Chambersburg PA
CBHW070113230526
45472CB00004B/1234